# Collins *rambl*

C000003744

# connemara

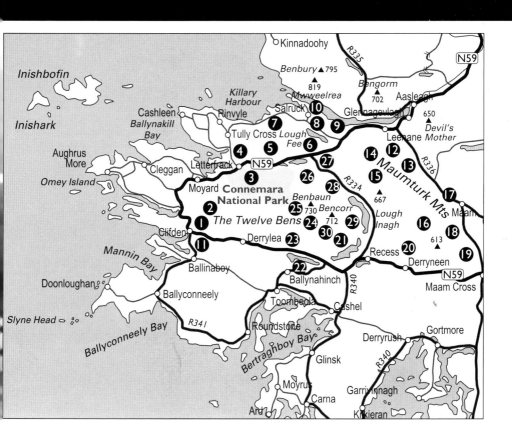

The Ramblers' Association, because it does not have a presence in Ireland, has not been able to check the text or maps in this book. Therefore, unlike most other titles in this series, the Association can take no responsibility for the accuracy of the walks provided. It endorses the series as a whole and fully expects this volume to be of an equally high standard to that of the other titles in the series.

HarperCollins*Publishers*
77–85 Fulham Palace Road
London
W6 8JB

The HarperCollins website address is:

www.**fire**and**water**.com

Collins is a registered trademark of HarperCollins*Publishers* Ltd.

First published 2001

06  05  04  03  02  01

10  9  8  7  6  5  4  3  2  1

The author asserts his moral right to be identified as the author of this work.
All rights reserved

HarperCollins*Publishers* would like to thank Michael Gibbons from the Connemara
Walking Centre for checking the walks and for providing the information and photos in
Walk 11.

Series Editor Richard Sale

© in this edition HarperCollins*Publishers*
© in text and photographs Paddy Dillon
© in the maps Harvey Map Services Ltd., Doune, Perthshire
Title page map © Bartholomew Ltd. 2001

ISBN 0 00 220121 6

Designed and produced by Drum Enterprises Ltd.
Printed and bound in Great Britain by Scotprint

# CONTENTS

# How to use this book

This book contains route maps and descriptions for 30 walks. Each walk is graded (see p.3) and areas of interest are indicated by symbols (see below). For each walk particular points of interest are denoted by a capital letter both in the text and on the map (where the letter appears in a red box). In the text the route descriptions are prefixed by lower-case letters. We recommend that you read the whole description, including the tinted box at the start of each walk, before setting out.

# Key to maps

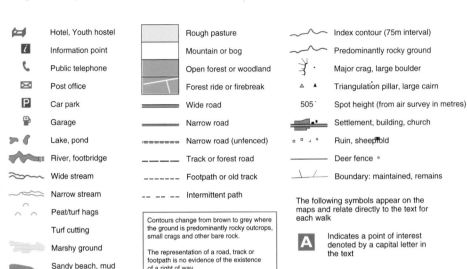

| | Hotel, Youth hostel | | Rough pasture | | Index contour (75m interval) |
| | Information point | | Mountain or bog | | Predominantly rocky ground |
| | Public telephone | | Open forest or woodland | | Major crag, large boulder |
| | Post office | | Forest ride or firebreak | | Triangulation pillar, large cairn |
| | Car park | | Wide road | 505 | Spot height (from air survey in metres) |
| | Garage | | Narrow road | | Settlement, building, church |
| | Lake, pond | | Narrow road (unfenced) | | Ruin, sheepfold |
| | River, footbridge | | Track or forest road | | Deer fence |
| | Wide stream | | Footpath or old track | | Boundary: maintained, remains |
| | Narrow stream | | Intermittent path | | |
| | Peat/turf hags | | | | |
| | Turf cutting | | | | |
| | Marshy ground | | | | |
| | Sandy beach, mud | | | | |
| | Island, coastal rock | | | | |

Contours change from brown to grey where the ground is predominantly rocky outcrops, small crags and other bare rock.

The representation of a road, track or footpath is no evidence of the existence of a right of way.

On moorland, walls, ruined walls and fences are shown. For farmland, only the outer boundary wall or fence is shown.

The following symbols appear on the maps and relate directly to the text for each walk

**A** Indicates a point of interest denoted by a capital letter in the text

**a** Indicates route instruction denoted by a lower-case letter in the text

Please note the scale for maps is 1:40,000 unless otherwise stated (25mm on the map represents 1,000m on the ground). North is always at the top of the page.

**scale 1:40 000** 25mm on the map represents 1000m on the ground

0 Kilometres          1          2          3

0 Miles          1          2

# Key to symbols

The walks in this book are graded from 1–5 according to the level of difficulty, with 1 being the easiest and 5 the most difficult. We recommend that walks graded 4 or higher (or grade 3 where indicated) should only be undertaken by experienced walkers who are competent in the use of map and compass and who are aware of the difficulties of the terrain they will encounter. The use of detailed maps is recommended for all routes.

At the start of each walk there is a series of symbols that indicate particular areas of interest associated with the route.

 Geology

 Birdlife

 Other wildlife

 Wild flowers

 Literature

 Good views

 Historical interest

 Woodland

# INTRODUCTION

Connemara is that rugged portion of West Galway, bounded on three sides by the sea. Galway Bay marks its southern extent, while the fjord-like Killary Harbour is its northern boundary. A spread of islands on its Atlantic coast are included, while its eastern limits are traditionally Joyce's River, the Maum Valley and Lough Corrib. 'Gateways to Connemara' include places such as Leenane and Oughterard. The nearest city is Galway, while Clifden is generally regarded as the 'capital' of Connemara.

The routes and maps in this guidebook are based on the area of covered by the Harveys Walker's Map of Connemara. This includes all the hills and mountains rising south of Killary Harbour, taking in the whole of the Twelve Bens and Maum Turk Mountain ranges; in effect covering all the mountainous parts of Connemara. The boggy southern parts of Connemara and its amazing spread of Atlantic islands are thus excluded, but the mountains feature some of the best and most challenging walks in the region.

## GEOLOGY

An amazingly complex and contorted geology owes it foundations to a collision of continents, when Pre-Cambrian and Cambrian sediments were folded and faulted in a period of mountain building. Intrusive masses of gabbro were pushed from deep within the earth, baking the surrounding bedrock. Extreme temperatures and pressures squeezed and distorted beds of sandstones, mudstones and limestones, changing them by a process of metamorphism into quartzites, schists and marbles. Another succession of sediments were laid down in the Ordovician and Silurian periods, which have themselves undergone complex folding and faulting, though without any accompanying metamorphism. An extensive granitic intrusion was later pushed into the bedrock, again baking and distorting the already much disturbed strata. The most recent occurrence, in geological time, was the Ice Age, when the mountains gave birth to glaciers which flowed relentlessly downhill, carving out high corries, deep glacial valleys and the fjord-like inlet of Killary Harbour.

The end result for walkers is an intriguingly varied group of mountains. In north Connemara, alongside Killary Harbour,

An extremely coarse boulder conglomerate at Maolchnoc. Note the scale provided by the water bottle in the middle.

are the Ordovician and Silurian sedimentary series, with their steeply dipping beds. Dúchruach is made of the dark gabbro intrusion and it dominates the area around Kylemore. In the central parts of Connemara, the Twelve Bens are mostly composed of bright quartzite, though Meacanach is a prominent mountain of schist. The Maum Turk Mountains are also quartzite, and like the Twelve Bens show plenty of evidence of glaciation. The thin and disjointed marble beds lie along the southern flanks of the Twelve Bens, often evidenced by lighter green areas of grass. Progressing further southwards onto Roundstone Bog, the landscape is mostly granitic and low in altitude.

## HUMAN OCCUPATION AND HISTORY

A recent find of an arrowhead has taken the human occupation of Connemara back over 7,000 years. The area at that time would have been well forested, with only the higher rocky peaks protruding. The first hunter gatherers did not venture far inland, and the only traces they left were occasional midden sites. A concerted push into the forest was made around 6,000 years ago by a well organised people who created areas for agriculture by hacking back and burning the forest. They also left impressive tombs, dating back over 5,000 years. A change in the climate, possibly created by their ruthless attack on the forest, seems to have been their downfall. Wet conditions led to the soil becoming waterlogged and mossy, leading to the inexorable growth of extensive blanket bogs. In many areas, signs of human occupation became completely engulfed by the bogs and are only today being unearthed. In a drier period, the bog seems to have become extensively forested in Scots Pine, before the return of another wetter period.

During the Bronze Age, well-organised communities living around the fringes of the mountains of Connemara erected a series of spectacular monuments. Stone rows and standing stones are thought to have had particular alignments and may have been used to keep track of the changing seasons. The Winter Solstice seems to have been a particularly important time. Moving into the Iron Age, the communities seem to have been smaller and more likely to be organised in defensive groupings. A number of earthen ring forts or stone cashels date from this period, and indeed lasted into early Christian times.

The name Connemara derives from the people known as the Conmaicne Mara, who claimed descent from Fergus Mac Roi of

A 'crannog' or artificial lake-island dwelling. This example is at the Connemara Heritage and History Centre.

A reconstructed 'ringfort' with huts encircled by a palisade. Thousands of these have been identified in Ireland.

Ulster and Queen Medbh of Connacht, which would give the name a currency of nearly 2,000 years. Whatever their origins, the Conmaicne Mara lived through a Christian conversion and Viking raids, then were gradually supplanted by the O'Flaherty clan; particularly in the 13th Century when the Anglo-Norman Burkes took control of all the O'Flaherty's eastern territories. The O'Flaherty's were fierce and warlike, but seemed to spend as much time fighting among themselves as fighting outsiders. People used to pray for deliverance from the 'Fury of the O'Flaherty's'. The islands were for a time under the control of the 16th Century sea-queen Gráinne Mhael, who married into the O'Flaherty clan and obtained some mainland territories.

Despite the bleakness of its terrain, Connemara came under considerable population pressure during the strife associated with the 17th-Century Cromwellian campaigns. Soldiers and adventurers were rewarded with land confiscated in the area, while the dispossessed from all over Ireland were told to go 'To Hell or Connacht', so that a steady flow of refugees spilled into the area. Some of the O'Flaherty's fought on the side of the monarchy and lost property, if not their lives, but seldom was any property returned on the restoration of Charles II.

Dan O'Hara's Cottage at the Connemara Heritage and History Centre is typical of the early 19th Century.

Some of the first topographical descriptions of Connemara were penned by the historian Roderick O'Flaherty, including descriptions of the Twelve Bens and Maum Turk Mountains. 'On the north-west of Balynahinsy,' he wrote, 'are the twelve high mountains of Bennabeola, called by mariners the twelve stakes, being the first land they discover as they come from the maine. Bindowglass is the highest of them, and, next the lake, is two miles high; and hath standing water on the top of it, wherein they say if any washeth his head, he becomes hoare.'

The Maum Turk Mountains were also mentioned by O'Flaherty, who explained, '... the passes that open through are called Mam, as Mam-eich, Mam-tuirk, and Mam-en. There is a well in memorie of St. Fechin at Mam-tuirk. At Mam-en, there springs out of a stone a litle water, named from St. Patrick, which is a present remedy against murrein in cattel, not only applyed, but alsoe as soon as tis sent for they begin to have ease. Next Mam-en are the mountains of Corcoga, in the confines of Balynahynsy, Ross, and Moycullin countreys, where the fat deere is frequently hunted; whereof no high mountain in the barony of Balynahinsy, or half barony of Rosse, is destitude.'

It was around this time that the Martin family came to hold a vast portion of Connemara. They claimed the longest driveway in the world, from Galway city to the door of Ballynahinch Castle. Many of the members were larger than life, including the lawyer 'Nimble' Dick, who held onto the property throughout the Williamite campaigns. The last notable member was 'Hairtrigger' Dick, who was a master duellist, but was latterly remembered as 'Humanity' Dick for his concern for animal welfare. As a Member of Parliament he brought into being an Act outlawing cruelty to animals. He was also a great spender of money and during his years the estates in Connemara became bankrupt and he died penniless in Boulogne after fleeing from creditors.

Early writers commented on the formidable wildness of Connemara. 'I never saw so strangely stony and wild a country,' wrote a Mr. Molyneaux in 1709. 'I did not see all this way three living creatures, not one house or ditch, not one bit of corn, nor, I may say, one bit of land, for stones, in short nothing appeared but stones and sea. Nor could I conceive an inhabited country so destitute of all signs of people.' John Millington Synge penned much the same sentiments, saying, 'the fields looked so small and rocky that the very thought of tillage in them seemed like the freak of an eccentric.'

The town of Clifden was founded in 1812, but during the dark years of the Great Famine, 1845–8, progress in the area seemed to grind to a halt and the countryside was depopulated by starvation and death, eviction and emigration. What emerged from those years was a Connemara which is recognisable to today's traveller. Relief work was instituted in the region, notably at Letterfrack, and roads were built to provide employment. In 1895 the Galway to Clifden Railway was open and tourism began to develop apace. While the area

Kylemore Post Office. One of many structures attesting to the improvement in rural services late in the 19th Century.

saw little action during the Easter Rising of 1916, there were numerous skirmishes and shootings in the 'Troubles' of the 1920s. With fishing, farming, industry and tourism all shifting gradually forwards, today's Connemara has emerged from 7,000 years of human activity.

## NATURAL HISTORY

Human impact on the development of the Connemara landscape must always be taken into account. There is a school of thought suggesting that the growth of extensive blanket bogs, which smother the mountains and glens of Connemara, may in part have been due to man's folly in felling the great forests of the region. Whatever the truth, the bogs are an absorbing study in their own right. Learned studies have analysed the pollen caught in layer upon layer of humic material and reconstructed a landscape of constant botanical change.

Woodlands are rare in today's landscape. The deciduous woods at Kylemore are secondary plantings, and the nature reserve beside Derryclare Lough is best described as semi-natural. A few gnarled trees clinging to cliffs appear to be all that is left of the great forests, while plants such as wood sorrel have adapted to the shade provided by rocky crevices and boulders. The broad bogs are extensively covered in purple moor grass, which largely determines the colour of Connemara throughout the seasons. Heather is seldom extensive, though it is widespread. Huge areas of bogland have become blotted out with the plantation of ugly coniferous stands.

In the mountains, an amazing variety of plants cling to bare rock and scree for survival. A small number of Alpine plants are to be found, most notably on the steep-sided mountain of Meacanach in the Twelve Bens. On almost all the mountains specimens of the Hiberno-Lusitanian St. Patrick's Cabbage can be found. Hardy thrift forms compact cushions, and creeping juniper and crowberry can be spotted in the uncompromisingly rocky terrain. A heather peculiar to the region is St. Dabeoc's Heath, another Hiberno-Lusitanian, while even rarer heathers can be located by venturing across Roundstone Bog.

While a variety of birds can be spotted, there are unlikely to be great numbers noticed in any one day. Woodlands offer the best chances of recording a variety of species. Some birds are quite restricted to certain habitats, such as mountain slopes or bogland, where few species are ever noted. Mammals are few in number and mostly very secretive. While red deer are being reintroduced to the area, the walker is unlikely to spot anything larger than a fox or Irish hare, though there are rare pine marten to be observed and a variety of bats. Many birds and mammals represented in Britain and Europe simply do not exist in Ireland, or may be absent or uncommon in Connemara. Abundant fox moth caterpillars are likely to be noted grazing the grassy bogs, and the same bogs are ideal breeding territory for the voracious midge! Frogs and newts represent the amphibian wildlife, while snakes are, of course, absent.

A visit to the Connemara National Park visitor centre is advised for walkers who have a particular interest in the natural history of Connemara. Park staff have access to up-to-date records of what is growing or moving through the area.

## WALKING IN CONNEMARA

Early written references are to be treated with great caution whenever distances are mentioned, owing to the usage of the 'magnis milliaribus Conaciensibus' or 'long Connacht miles' which seem to have been anything up to two statute miles! Walkers may indeed feel that the distances in this guidebook are based on the same 'long miles', but it is more likely that the rugged nature of the terrain is to blame for any lost time.

Today's walker will be able to enjoy studying the amazingly contorted geology of Connemara, as well as enquiring into its long history. It is possible to find remnant Arctic-Alpine plants growing beside Hiberno-Lusitanian flora, and the buried remains of pine stumps in awesome blanket bogs which have been growing since the Bronze Age. A series of visitor and heritage centres allow interested walkers to enquire into the background of Connemara; its archaeology, history, natural history, life and work. The walks include opportunities to visit the tiny Connemara National Park, the impressive Kylemore Abbey, the Connemara Heritage and History Centre, the Leenane Cultural Centre and the little Quiet Man Cottage.

Walkers who can find their way across bleak, remote, rocky and pathless terrain can head for the heights and find their own way around, but there are also a few low-level walks on clear paths and tracks. Signposts for walkers are rare, but there is a high degree of access by permission of landowners. Easy guided walks can be sampled at the Connemara National Park, while in Clifden there is a Connemara Walking Centre offering maps, guidebooks, guided walks and plenty of practical advice. Clifden is host to a number of Walking Festivals where expert local guides will help all comers to enjoy the delights of walking in Connemara. Seldom have walkers had it so good!

The 30 routes in this guidebook have been chosen to illustrate the amazing variety of the area. There are several fine upland walks in the Twelve Bens and Maum Turk Mountains, including some very rugged, rocky routes. There are many gentler hill walks, some with clear paths, but others being pathless. A number of low-level walks wander alongside rivers or wrap themselves around sprawling loughs.

While enjoying the range of walks, there are comments on the underlying geology or land use; notes about the flora or fauna which might be seen; a mention of nearby facilities offering

food or drink; or simply a description of the extensive views, which are best observed in the sunny spells immediately following a shower of rain. Snow and frost are rare in Connemara, so even in winter it is possible to walk for longer without recourse to winter walking equipment, or ice axe and crampon skills. Mist, however, is very common, and the more

Walkers who can find their way across bleak, remote, rocky and pathless terrain can head for the heights.

Snow and frost are rare in Connemara, so it is possible to walk for longer without recourse to winter equipment.

remote and rugged a walk is, the more the walker needs to be able to use a map and compass accurately. Remember, trodden paths are few, and even where they do occur they can be vague and discontinuous. Sheep rearing is an important occupation and wire fencing is becoming increasingly common on the mountains. Sometimes the fences provide a useful guide across featureless terrain, but at other times they almost make a walk into a hurdling event. Most prominent fences are mentioned in the route descriptions.

## SERVICES

The main N59 road curves through Connemara and provides access to most of the walks; from Maam Cross to Clifden and from Clifden to Leenane. The only other roads which are used to any extent are the R344, from Kylemore to Recess and the R336 road from Leenane to Mám and Maam Cross. Minor roads around Letterfrack, Lettergesh and Killary Harbour complete the picture. There have been no rail services in Connemara since 1935, with public transport being provided by two bus companies. Bus Éireann (referred to locally as the CIE bus) operates between Galway and Clifden, with some services routed via the Maum Valley and Leenane. The Connemara Bus (referred to locally as Michael Nee's bus) also operates between Galway and Clifden, with links to some outlying villages and an occasional service to Letterfrack. There are plenty of buses in the summer months, but considerably less in the winter. Always check timetable details carefully with the operators if relying on these services.

Scottish Blackface sheep are contained by wire fencing, both on the increase and an unhappy combination in this instance.

While settlements are sparsely scattered throughout the upland regions of Connemara, there is abundant accommodation. Clifden is the most obvious centre and has the greatest choice, but there are plenty of other places to stay. Caravan and campsites are few and there are only two An Óige Youth Hostels. There are a handful of independent hostels, self-catering cottages, numerous B&Bs and guest houses, and several fine hotels to choose from. In the peak summer period it is wise to book beds in advance, but conversely, places begin to close down during the winter. If the museums or visitor centres are to be visited, it should be noted that some of these close for the winter too. Full details can be checked in the Tourist Information Centre in Clifden during the summer, but in winter checking would need to be done through the Tourist Information Centre in Galway.

Walkers who require specific information about walking routes in Connemara, or who require the services of a guide, should contact Michael Gibbons of the Connemara Walking Centre in Clifden. Michael's enthusiasm and assistance in the preparation of this guidebook are gratefully acknowledged.

# OWENGLIN RIVER AND CLIFDEN

**START:**
On the concrete bridge over the Owenglin River at Barr na nÓrán. A lift to this point should be arranged if possible.

**FINISH:**
Clifden, though it is also possible to call for a taxi from the Clifden Glen Holiday Village, to avoid ending with a road walk.

**DISTANCE:** 6 miles (9.5km).

**APPROXIMATE TIME:** 3 hours.

**HIGHEST POINT:** 300ft (100m) at the start at Barr na nÓrán.

**MAPS:** Harveys Superwalker Connemara; OS Sheet 37.

**REFRESHMENTS:**
Clifden Glen Holiday Village has a bar and restaurant, and there are many more places offering food and drink in Clifden.

**ADVICE:**
A walk along a river such as the Owenglin could be considered as a low-level walk in bad weather, but remember that there are a couple of inflowing streams to cross, which may be swollen after heavy rain. Fences can sometimes be quite close to the river, especially near the start.

The Owenglin is the river running from the Twelve Bens to Clifden. It is a true mountain river, a rushing torrent after heavy rain, with powerful waterfalls plunging into rocky gorges. There are a handful of farmsteads along its course, and for most of the way there is a fence alongside the river, so that the walk is essentially confined to a strip of ground beside the water. The route is linear, and it seems best to walk in the direction of Clifden in order to finish with its full range of facilities. It is therefore necessary to arrange for a lift to Barr na nÓrán to start the walk.

## A  Barr na nÓrán 744513

Anglicised as Barnanoraun, Barr na nÓrán means the Top of the Spring Wells. Green-banded ornamental Connemara Marble at Barr na nÓrán has been quarried since the 1820s. The first quarry was started by Thomas Martin of Ballynahinch Castle. The marble appears as a variable band in highly contorted strata, often proving difficult to locate and exploit at times.

**a**  Access to Barr na nÓrán is via a narrow, dead-end road from the main N59 road between Clifden and Benlettery Youth Hostel. If a lift can be arranged to the concrete bridge over the Owenglin River, then the river can be followed back towards Clifden, with no need to retrieve a car afterwards. Just before the bridge, walk downstream, but note that at first there is only a narrow strip of grassy ground between the fence and the river. There is rather more space later, so be patient and persevere! There are two farmsteads standing close to the river and the enclosed fields are used primarily for sheep-grazing. Looking back, note the fine views around the mountains, all part of the Twelve Bens, which surround the head of the glen. The steep-sided glen was carved out by glacial action during the Ice Age.

**b**  After passing the second farm, the rushing river is augmented by a stream flowing from Loch na hUilleann. In wet weather, expect wet feet while fording the channel. Cross a stile over a fence which runs into the Owenglin River, then continue downstream. There are a couple of fine waterfalls, which are followed by a more spectacular fall at Eas Mór.

## B   Eas Mór 719510

Eas Mór translates as the Big Waterfall, where the Owenglin pours over a rockstep into a rocky gorge. There is a spike of rock to be passed before the water can leave the gorge. Look out for a variety of birds, including the dipper, wheatear and skylark. Look back upstream for another fine view of the Twelve Bens. Closer to hand, note the shrubs which have gained a roothold on the rock walls, such as oak, holly and ivy. The moorland slopes bear grass, heather and a ground scrub of gorse.

The Owenglin flows westwards from Barr na nÓrán with the Twelve Bens forming a wonderful backdrop.

**c**   There are fairly placid meanders along the river. The route passes close to Cregg Lough, but this is out of sight over a heathery rise just to the north. The TV masts on top of Cregg Hill are occasionally in view though. Staying close to the river leads to another splendid waterfall called Eas Beag.

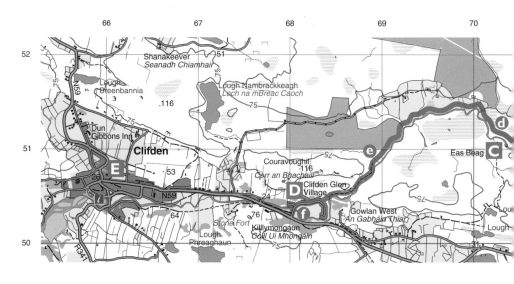

## C   Eas Beag 703512

Eas Beag, or the Little Waterfall, is where the Owenglin splits into two channels around a rocky island.

Eas Beag translates as the Little Waterfall, and yet it is a powerful display. The Owenglin splits into two around a rocky island, with fine waterfalls on both sides. One fall is broad and easily visible, while the other is narrow and falls into a hidden undercut slit.

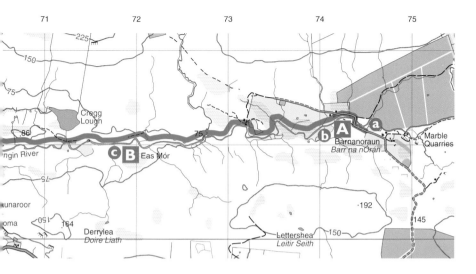

**d** Continue downstream, passing a sheep pen and taking care across marshy, rushy ground where an inflowing stream from Cregg Lough joins the Owenglin. There is a steep and rugged slope clothed in bracken to cross, then an easier grassy stretch follows. The route passes below a couple more farmsteads at Tooraskeheen, then runs beside a recent forest plantation which has had a margin of young oak trees placed alongside.

**e** Cross a stile over a fence at the edge of the forest and walk across a boggy slope. Don't follow the river through a constricted valley, but climb uphill a little to locate a narrow, gravel path. Signs may be spotted pointing off to the right, but the path should be followed downstream, to the left, roughly parallel to the Owenglin. Boggy grass and heather slopes, with bog myrtle and abundant gorse scrub, are passed. There is a last chance to look back towards the Twelve Bens before they pass from sight. The path leads downhill, crossing a footbridge to reach the Clifden Glen Holiday Village.

### D  Clifden Glen Holiday Village 683505
A multitude of chalets appears quite suddenly beside the Owenglin. This is the Clifden Glen Holiday Village. While it was being developed, gnarled, well-established oak trees were incorporated into the layout of the place. Non-residents are welcome and the site boasts a restaurant and bar, tennis court, pitch and putt, with angling also available.

A more placid stretch of the Owenglin flows past a couple of small farmsteads at Tooraskeheen.

**f** The access road from Clifden Glen crosses the Owenglin River and joins the main N59 road. A right turn leads straight back towards Clifden, and the road also has an occasional bus service. A taxi into town could be arranged by phoning from Clifden Glen. Anyone who has parked a car at the start of the walk at Barr na nÓrán will need to arrange for its collection by organising a lift.

### E Clifden 657507

Clifden is a small market town which was founded by John D'Arcy in 1812. It grew rapidly in the first half of the 19th Century and is therefore one of the youngest towns in Ireland; John D'Arcy's home was at Clifden Castle, a Gothic structure which is now in ruins out along the Sky Road. A monument in memory of John D'Arcy stands on the brow of a hill just to the west of town. A beautiful view of the town, with its two church spires and a backdrop of the Twelve Bens can be seen from it. During the 'Troubles' in 1921, the hanging of a Clifden-born 'Volunteer' was followed by the IRA shooting dead two RIC constables. This in turn was followed by the Black and Tans storming the town, burning houses and killing one of the inhabitants. Services include a full range of accommodation options, shops, pubs and restaurants. Be sure to visit the Connemara Walking Centre, which offers information about walking opportunities in the area, as well as guided walks and tours for groups and individuals. Clifden hosts events such as an Arts Festival, Connemara Pony shows and sales, and interesting Walking Festivals. The town has witnessed two historic transatlantic links with America: Marconi was in radio communication between his station at Clifden and one in Nova Scotia from 1907. Alcock & Brown's non-stop transatlantic flight ended abruptly in the bog alongside the radio station in 1909. After the shooting dead of two IRA men near the station, the place was attacked and burnt to the ground in 1922, never to reopen.

The chalets at the Clifden Glen Holiday Village have been constructed around stands of gnarled oak trees.

# CIRCUIT OF CREGG HILL

**START/FINISH:**
On the higher parts of the minor, dead-end road serving the TV masts on Cregg Hill. Note that there are only small parking spaces beside the road. Access is from the main N59 road at Rosleague.

**DISTANCE:** 4½ miles (7km).

**APPROXIMATE TIME:** 2½ hours.

**HIGHEST POINT:** 967ft (297m) on the summit of Cregg Hill.

**MAPS:** Harveys Superwalker Connemara; OS Sheet 37.

**REFRESHMENTS:**
None on the route, but there are places to eat and drink around Letterfrack and Moyard on the main N59 road afterwards.

**ADVICE:**
The walk around Cregg Hill is rough, wet and pathless, but there are some good guiding features such as forest fences and another fence leading all the way to the summit. Cregg Hill has road access all the way to its summit.

It is possible to drive all the way to the summit of Cregg Hill, or at least so close that the walk to the summit is a mere detail. No other hilltop in Connemara is quite so accessible. The narrow road running to the summit TV masts starts on the main N59 road, at Rosleague, between Letterfrack and Moyard. There are a few points of interest around this short walk. One is the fine view of the Twelve Bens from close quarters; another is a marble quarry which is only occasionally in use; and there is also an abandoned farming settlement near Cregg Lough. A short, rugged, circular hill walk combines all three points.

Looking across Loch na hUilleann from the slopes of Cregg Hill, with the rugged face of An Chailleach beyond.

## A   Cregg Hill 715525

Cregg Hill is only a lowly eminence at 967ft (297m) but it is easily recognised in many Connemara views because of the twin TV masts on its summit. Its Irish name is An Chreig, meaning simply The Crag. The only sizeable crag on the hill is the one above the marble quarry on the approach road. The marble quarry is only rarely in operation, while the rusting sheds and machinery associated with it contribute nothing to the scenic merits of the area. Although referred to as a quarry, the marble is actually mined from caverns.

Either walk alongside the forest fence, or on the lower slopes of Cregg Hill, but keep off the broad bogland.

**a**   Parking is very limited beside the approach road, so perhaps it is best to drive to the summit, then turn around and select one of the small roadside spaces on the way back down. Start walking down the narrow tarmac road, enjoying fine views of the Twelve Bens across Loch na hUilleann.

## B   Loch na hUilleann 725533

Anglicised as Lough Nahillion, Loch na hUilleann is the Lake of the Elbow. There is one pine-clad island, one peninsula and four other little islands, appearing like giant stepping stones leading towards the Twelve Bens.

**b**   Walk a short way past the Marble Quarry, whose gates are flanked with forbidding notices, and cross a fence on the left of the road to walk across an area of bog beside a forest. Walk

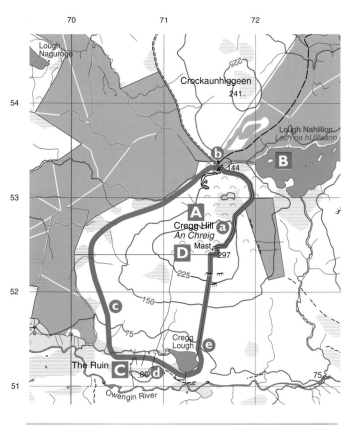

A roofless ruin is all that remains of a small farmstead where an area of fertile limestone grassland was exploited.

alongside the forest fence, studying the pock-marked, quarried face of Cregg Hill to the left. There is a turf bank beside a small stream, with another fence to cross. It is possible to walk alongside the forest fence, or to walk on the other side of a broad area of bog, staying on the lower slopes of Cregg Hill. Don't walk too far out onto the level parts of the bog, which can be very soft and wet in places. Notice the appearance of heather, purple moor grass and bog myrtle.

c   After turning gradually around the lower slopes of Cregg Hill, there is a view into a small, boggy valley. Looking across the valley, there is an elongated, low green hill, with a few trees along its base and the ruin of an old farmhouse on top. Walk towards this hill and pick a way up its rocky slopes to reach the farmhouse. There is a fence to cross in the valley and another to cross just before reaching the ruin. The bedrock is a strangely fluted limestone, metamorphosed almost to marble, which affects the nature of the terrain and the vegetation in the area around the ruined farmhouse.

## C   The Ruin 707513

The ruined farmstead has a number of nearby outbuildings; including some at the foot of the cliff. There is an old limekiln and the remains of drystone walls around former fields. A 'killeen', or children's burial ground, and a Holy Well are located nearby. As the bedrock is limestone and the land has been well-cultivated in the past, the vegetation is remarkably different to that on the surrounding boggy moorlands. Note the buttercups, dandelions, clover, plantain, nettles, ragwort, ox-eye daisies, wild iris, wood sorrel, bracken, hartstongue fern and gnarled hawthorns. All these plants are absent from the bleak and barren moorland slopes of Cregg Hill.

d   Leaving the limestone hill, walk on a boggy, heathery crest just to the south of Cregg Lough. This is the mallard's natural habitat. Note the fine view of the Twelve Bens across the water, and also note the line of a fence which runs straight from the shore of the lough to the TV masts on the summit of Cregg Hill.

e   Follow the fence uphill. The first part of the boggy slope ends abruptly at a sheer rock outcrop. Holly, ivy, bramble, spleenwort and willow trees are in abundance. Step to the right to find a breach in the cliff, which has been used by sheep, then follow the fence further uphill. The ground steepens towards the top, but the TV masts remain in view. The fence crosses over a heathery dome, and, after crossing

An unmistakable guide in any weather; the line of a fence runs up to the TV masts on the top of Cregg Hill.

another fence at a junction, the part of the hill bearing the TV masts is reached. Just to one side, a small cairn marks the true natural summit of Cregg Hill.

### D   The View from Cregg Hill 715525

Despite the intrusive nature of the TV masts, there is a good all round view from the top of Cregg Hill, stretching far and near. Look out for distant Achill Island and the Nephin Beg Range, with Diamond Hill, Dúchruach and the Twelve Bens closer to hand. The Bens include Cnoc Breac, An Chailleach, Meacanach, Binn Bhán, Binn Dhubh, Binn Bhraoin, Binn Gabhar and Binn Ghleann Uisce. More distant again are Cashel Hill, Errisbeg and Tully Mountain, with parts of the coastline and the lake-strewn Roundstone Bog featuring in intricate detail.

# DIAMOND HILL, CONNEMARA NATIONAL PARK

**D**iamond Hill must be the hill most often climbed in Connemara. It lies within easy reach of the Connemara National Park Visitor Centre at Letterfrack and has an imposing profile. The park staff do not encourage visitors to climb Diamond Hill, pointing out that the path to the summit, as well as paths on the flanks of the hill, are becoming badly eroded. However, they do not actually prevent anyone from making the climb. Thousands of walkers make the ascent each year. Anyone who is looking for a quiet hill walk in summer will find that there are plenty of other good alternatives around Connemara. The route described here makes a direct ascent, then returns through the boggy Gleann Mhór and skirts around the lower flanks of the hill.

## A Visitor Centre 712574

In 1974 the Christian Brothers left Letterfrack and the Archbishop of Tuam prepared to sell the grim Industrial School and the estate around it. Most of the land was acquired by the Office of Public Works in 1976, so that it could be developed into a small National Park; a mere 8 square miles. The land included Diamond Hill and its surroundings. The old infirmary now serves as the Park Administration office, while the farm buildings have been converted into the exhibition and reception areas. The old reservoir has been preserved: its waters were harnessed for

**START/FINISH:**
At the Connemara National Park Visitor Centre, reached by a signposted access road from the main N59 road near Letterfrack, between Clifden and Kylemore. There is a charge for parking.

**DISTANCE:** 5 miles (8km).

**APPROXIMATE TIME:** 3 hours.

**HIGHEST POINT:** 1460ft (440m) on the summit of Diamond Hill.

**MAPS:** Harveys Superwalker Connemara; OS Sheet 37.

**REFRESHMENTS:**
The National Park Visitor Centre has a restaurant and there are other places offering food and drink within easy walking distance at Letterfrack.

**ADVICE:**
A popular climb, but accomplished on badly eroded peaty paths. Expect to find wet and muddy ground.

The Connemara National Park visitor centre is based in farm buildings belonging to the former Industrial School.

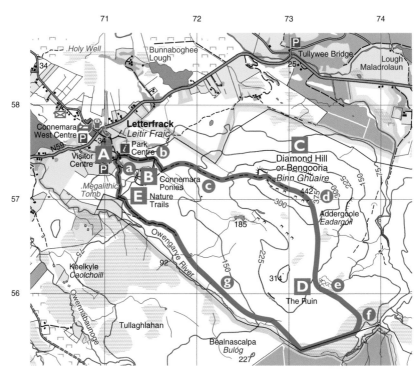

Walkers start climbing up the rugged slopes of Diamond Hill after leaving the Sruffaunboy Nature Trail.

power in 1925, bringing electricity to the Industrial School and Letterfrack. The Visitor Centre includes displays about the flora and fauna of the Connemara National Park and there is an audio visual theatre alongside. Informative guided walks are sometimes led by the Park Rangers, especially during the summer months.

**a** There are a couple of nature trails leaving the Visitor Centre. Follow the Sruffaunboy Nature Trail, which is marked by a prominent stone block between the Visitor Centre and the Park administration office. Pass through a little wooden gate beside a large iron gate, following a gravel track gently uphill with gorse and brambles to the left and a fenced paddock to the right. There are Connemara Ponies in the paddock.

### B Connemara Ponies 712575
The Connemara Pony is best described as being a small horse. It is a tough breed well able to cope with life in rugged Connemara. It is said that native ponies were crossed with horses and ponies from Spain and Morocco to produce the

Connemara Pony. The breed was almost lost in recent decades, but careful stock selection has retained and developed its traits. Lord Killanin is a notable supporter of the breed. Colours range from dappled grey, through many hues of brown, to black. They are considered friendly and easy to handle, a favourite with children and possessed of an intelligence that favours them for dressage and show events. Ponies bred and reared in the Connemara National Park have the word 'Park' included in their names.

**b**   Another little wooden gate beside another large iron gate is passed through to reach stop Number 4 on the nature trail. There is a view to the left over Ballynakill Harbour, then the gravel path swings to the right. Turn off the path almost immediately to the left, following a trodden path up a boggy slope towards Diamond Hill. Note the purple moor grass, bog myrtle, tormentil and heather.

**c**   The path is braided across the boggy slope and there are large boulders scattered around. Looking back, fine views open up towards the coast, taking in a spread of islands. The path steepens on a shoulder, being well worn in places and crossing stony ground and low rocky outcrops. There is a swing to the left on the steeper upper slopes, then there is a sudden view over a very steep slope to Kylemore Abbey and its surroundings. A broken ridge of hard quartzite and a very worn, peaty path lead to the summit cairn on Diamond Hill.

**C   Diamond Hill 732571**
Diamond Hill appears as a prominent rocky dome in many views, but its summit is fairly easy to reach at 1460ft (442m). Its Irish name of Binn Guaire is seldom used. Diamond Hill is comprehensively severed from the neighbouring Twelve Bens by the deeply-cut Polladirk River valley. Views embrace a fine stretch of the Connemara coast, including islands such as Inis Bó Finne, Inis Tuirc, Clare Island and Achill. Mountain groups include the Nephin Beg Range and Mweelrea. Also in view are Dúchruach, Binn Gorm, Devilsmother, Leenane Hill and Binn Bhriocáin. The Twelve Bens include Cnoc Breac, Binn Bhreac, Binn Bhán, Meacanach, and An Chailleach; all arranged around the glacial valley of Gleann Mhór. Errisbeg and Cregg Hill are lower eminences also in view. Crowberry, juniper and bearberry grow here and you are likely to spot a Raven or an Irish Hare.

**d**   Follow a narrower path away from the summit of Diamond Hill. This path is worn into the peaty slopes, then there is a gravelly stretch. Head off to the right and walk down to a broad

Looking from a window-hole at the ruined farmhouse, the distant dome of An Chailleach can be seen.

and boggy gap on the shoulder of Diamond Hill. Swing gradually to the left in a broad arc, crossing extensive slopes of grass and bog, to reach an isolated field system marked by a low stone ruin and a handful of trees.

### D   The Ruin 734562

The low stone ruin of a three-roomed farmstead can be investigated, along with its old field system. Clover and buttercups still grow in the remains of the improved pasture, which is now being invaded by rushes and is surrounded by extensive bogland. There are a mere handful of trees acting as landmarks on this bleak moorland slope. Sycamore, hawthorn and ash are a part of the landscape. The path which once connected the farmstead with Kylemore is now very difficult to trace across the rugged slopes of Diamond Hill.

**e** Descend from the old farmstead, through the old field system, where the ground can be quite uneven, to reach an area of sloping bogland beyond. Walk towards the boggy floor of Gleann Mhór, then head to the right towards the edge of a forest.

**f** Turn right to walk alongside the forest. The boggy ground is unremitting, and there are only vague paths along the way. Later, swing to the right to cross a boggy gap between Diamond Hill and Bealnascalpa. Here the path becomes much clearer on the ground: some parts are badly overtrodden. When an area of gorse bushes is reached, with a small waterfall off to the right, walk past some old turf cuttings to join a firmer gravel track. Watch out for a Stonechat or two!

Running in a short loop below the visitor centre, the Ellis Wood Nature Trail offers a short extension.

**g** The track is known as the Bog Road, and can be followed with greater ease back to the Visitor Centre. Hummocky, rugged, rocky, heathery and grassy slopes are crossed by the Bog Road. On the final descent to the Visitor Centre the track is enclosed by a variety of shrubs and trees.

### E Nature Trails 712574
There are two short nature trail loops which can be followed in a matter of minutes from the Visitor Centre. The Sruffaunboy Nature Trail loops around the lower slopes of Diamond Hill on a firm gravel track and is equipped with eleven numbered stops. The Ellis Wood Nature Trail loops downhill from the visitor centre through a flowery woodland, without formal numbered stops. Booklets detailing the diverse range of flora and fauna can be obtained from the reception desk in the visitor centre. Oak, ash, sycamore, elm, beech, rowan, bluebell, wild garlic, wood sorrel, primrose, wood avens, violet, golden saxifrage, ferns, mosses, and liverworts can all be found here. Birdlife in evidence here include the blue/great/coal and long-tailed tit, song/mistle thrush, treecreeper, robin, chaffinch, grey wagtail, hooded crow, cuckoo, fieldfare and wren.

# LETTERFRACK, DAWROS AND CURRYWONGAUN

**START/FINISH:**
At the crossroads in the centre of Letterfrack on the main N59 road between Leenane and Clifden. Parking is available beside Veldon's Bar and Restaurant.

**DISTANCE:** 8 miles (13km).

**APPROXIMATE TIME:** 4 hours.

**HIGHEST POINT:**
250ft (75m) on the lower slopes of Diamond Hill, unless the main road is used to return to Letterfrack, in which case the route does not exceed 150ft (50m).

**MAPS:** OS Sheet 37.

**REFRESHMENTS:**
There are bars and a restaurant in Letterfrack, as well as a restaurant attached to the Connemara National Park Visitor Centre.

**ADVICE:**
The route is basically low-level, easy and on firm surfaces, although the last stretch across the lower slopes of Diamond Hill can be wet and rugged. However, this slope can be avoided by returning via the main road.

An easy, low-level walk can be enjoyed almost any time and in any weather in the countryside around Letterfrack. Minor roads, a bog road and the possibility of a short stretch of rugged hillside can be combined in a circuit based on the village. Letterfrack owes its origins to James and Mary Ellis, Quaker settlers who provided employment, planted woodlands and constructed buildings in the area. Letterfrack is also important as the main entrance to the Connemara National Park. This walk ends with a more unorthodox entry to the National Park from the lower slopes of Diamond Hill.

## A   Letterfrack 799577

James and Mary Ellis were Quakers from Leicester in England, who arrived in Letterfrack in 1849, in the latter stages of the Great Famine. Stories of the hardship of the people had made a great impression on them and they resolved to improve conditions around Letterfrack. They bought an estate of 1800 acres of impoverished countryside, and embarked on a building project whose fruits can still be studied in the area around the village. These included a meeting house, school, temperance hotel, cottages, dispensary, shop and courthouse. Employment was provided for 80 people in building, farming, draining bogland and planting trees. Owing to the ill-health of James Ellis, the imaginative enterprise in Letterfrack came to an end in 1857. They sold out to John Hall, who was a supporter of the Irish Church Missionary Society. In 1882 the Christian Brothers bought the estate and were granted permission to create an 'Industrial School' in Letterfrack. Opened in 1887, this was the largest building in the village, it had five classrooms, three dormitories, a band room, kitchen, refectory, laundry and washrooms. There was room for over a hundred boys, with the Christian Brothers being housed in a small monastery alongside. The Industrial School closed in 1974 and the estate was broken up. Most of the land was purchased in 1976 to be developed as the Connemara National Park. In 1978 the main buildings of he Industrial School were purchased by Connemara West for use by the local community. The development includes a library, offices, surgery, radio station, meeting rooms, adult education classes, woodworking and design school, workshops, a farmer's co-op and a recreation hall – the latter named after James and Mary Ellis whose endeavours will long be remembered.

Diamond Hill towers over the former Industrial School at Letterfrack. The buildings now serve community needs.

**a** Leave the crossroads in Letterfrack by following the road signposted for Renvyle. When this road bends to the right, use a path and track on the left to cut out the bend and reach the Post Office by a direct line. Pass a road junction at Dawros, where the fuschia hedgerows screen rhododendron and invasive giant rhubarb. There is a grotto on the left before the open bog is reached.

**B  The Grotto 703583**
A plaque on the grotto reads: 'My name is Patrick Mortimer. I erected this grotto to Our Lady of Lourdes for been cured on

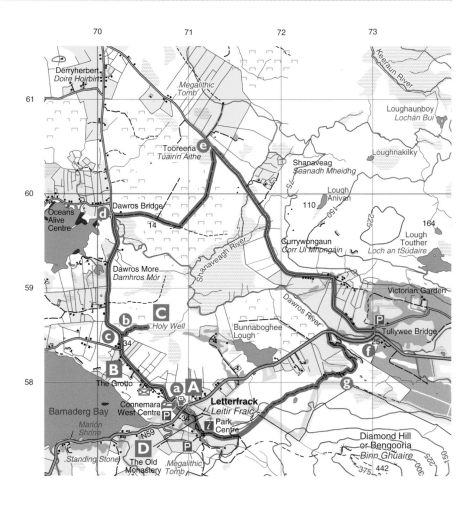

the 31 July 1980 and also for my son John. All thanks to Almighty God and Our Blessed Lady.'

**b** There is a fence to the right of the road and a grassy track leads down onto the bog. A walk along the track is an optional detour, leading alongside a rocky ridge to a Holy Well. The well is small and easily missed, being found shortly after the end of the track. There are a number of trees, shrubs and flowers to be noticed along the way, such as oak, rhododendron, hawthorn, holly, St. Dabeoc's Heath, heather and bog myrtle. Return to the road afterwards if this option is pursued, as there is no other easy way across the broad bog.

## C Holy Well 707586

The Holy Well is not easy to find, being located just beyond the end of the track at the foot of a rocky slope. A couple of stones have been set around it to define the tiny pool. It is associated with the local St. Ceannanach, who had his head cut off while visiting nearby Ballynew to the West. With apparent unconcern, he took his head to a Holy Well at Clooncree, where he washed it and set it back on his shoulders. Pausing only to curse the inhabitants of Ballynew he took his Christian message elsewhere.

c Follow the Renvyle road downhill and across a broad bogland, with fine views of Tully Mountain. Pass a reedy little lough, then cross Dawros Bridge. Note the old, grassy, double-arched stone bridge also spanning the tumultuous Dawros River and the presence of salmon, trout and otters.

d A stone proclaims 'Welcome to Renvyle Peninsula', but the route turns right along a gravel track, spurning the welcome for the time being. Follow the bog road past turf cuttings. Tully Mountain is now behind, while arranged in an arc all around are Mweelrea, Maolchnoc, Dúchruach, Maolan, Binn Bhreac, Cnoc Breac, Diamond Hill and Cregg Hill. Take the second track to the left and follow it further across the bog to reach a minor road.

e Turn right to follow the road, which is flanked by trees and shrubs: alder, holly, hawthorn, gorse, fuchsia, bramble and wild rose. The road runs gradually down to a bridge, with a couple of houses up to the left, against the mountainside. The road rises, banked by a stout retaining wall, crossing a shoulder before running past a number of houses. This area is called Currywongaun. Marconi briefly operated a radio station from 1913 on the hill above this settlement. There are plenty of mature trees on the way down to the main road, including beech, oak, rhododendron, scots pine. There is a huge Monterey Pine, with enormous spreading branches, which can be seen just before crossing Tullywee Bridge over the Dawros River.

f Turn right along the main N59 road, noting a huge bank of glacial drift. This is being gradually quarried away: the next turning left is an entrance for the quarry. While it is possible to follow the main road back to Letterfrack in a matter of a few minutes, there is an alternative off-road route too. The main road can be very busy in summer, though in winter it may be preferred to the wet and boggy slopes of Diamond Hill,

A grassy track leads across a rugged bogland to reach a tiny Holy Well associated with St. Ceannanach.

offering a drier return to Letterfrack. Take the next turning left after the quarry entrance. This track keeps to the right of the quarry, leading towards a farm at the foot of Diamond Hill. The farm is hidden in a stand of trees.

**g** Keep to the left before reaching the farm, cutting across a rugged, boggy slope to locate a small pool at the foot of Diamond Hill. There are only vague paths, nearly always wet underfoot, but by climbing slightly it is possible to cross a deer fence and drift up towards a corner on the Sruffaunboy Nature Trail in the Connemara National Park. Turn right to follow the trail downhill on a firm surface, passing through two gates to reach the Visitor Centre. Turn right at the centre, following a clear gravel track downhill from the Park Office. The track passes the Old Monastery Hostel, Catholic Church and Connemara West Centre to return to the crossroads in Letterfrack.

## D   The Old Monastery 711575

The Old Monastery was used by the Christian Brothers while they ran the Industrial School at Letterfrack. It now serves as an independent hostel. Apart from hostellers, the Old Monastery has a resident population of bats. Long-eared bats and Natterer's bats live together in the roofspace. Pipistrelle bats have also been recorded in the area, though they are not resident in the building.

The Dawros River is a powerful flow, well known to fishermen and a regular haunt of otters.

# KYLEMORE ABBEY AND DÚCHRUACH

**START/FINISH:**
Kylemore Abbey, which is between Leenane and Letterfrack on the main N59 road. There is a large car park at the entrance.

**DISTANCE:**
5½ miles (9km).

**APPROXIMATE TIME:** 3 hours.

**HIGHEST POINT:**
1736ft (526m) on the summit of Dúchruach.

**MAPS:** Harveys Superwalker Connemara; OS Sheet 37.

**REFRESHMENTS:**
The Kylemore Abbey Restaurant is located beside the car park.

**ADVICE:**
The walk up Dúchruach via the path described is fairly straightforward in clear weather. Note that other flanks of the hill are quite rugged and difficult to negotiate. Allow plenty of time to explore Kylemore Abbey, the Gothic Church and Lake Walk, as well as other attractions on the estate.

One of the most popular and most well-promoted images of Connemara is the view of Kylemore Abbey, seen across its lovely lough, with woodlands rising steeply behind. What is seldom seen is a view taking in rugged Dúchruach, at whose foot the Abbey was built. A moderate hill walk can take in the summit of Dúchruach, using a fine path most of the way. There is also the easy Lake Walk to consider, with its woodland trail, as well as an exploration of the Abbey and the delightful Gothic Church. This short walk seems to have everything! Mr and Mrs Hall wrote of their tour of Ireland in the *Parliamentary Gazette of Ireland* of 1843–44: 'The beautiful and magnificent pass of Kylemore fully equal in grandeur to the far-famed Gap of Dunloe in Kerry, or that of Barnesmore in Donegal, but possessing a beauty peculiarly its own.'

**A Kylemore Abbey 747585**
Kylemore Abbey was built as a residence for the wealthy Manchester merchant and philanthropist Mitchell Henry and his wife Margaret Vaughn. They had honeymooned in Kylemore in 1850 and bought an extensive holding in the area in 1862. Work on the building commenced in 1864, with the foundation stone being laid in 1867, from which grew the huge Gothic extravaganza. The estate boasted impressive gardens, glasshouses full of bananas, grapes and melons, lavish parties, an extensive staff, a model farm, stables and cottages. Tenants found Mitchell Henry to be a good landlord. The estate was purchased for the Duke and Duchess of Manchester in 1903, but was sold again in 1920 to the Irish Benedictine nuns. It is now an International Girls' Boarding School, and a magnet for tourists from around the world. A number of rooms are available for inspection by visitors, but not the school or the nun's quarters. Informative panels detail the history of the house, the history of the Benedictine Nuns, and there are items of furniture, pictures and other artefacts for study.

**a** Starting from the car park, enter the visitor centre to obtain a ticket and leaflets about the Abbey, Gothic Church and the Lake Walk. A video plays throughout the day in a building next to the Visitor Centre. The first objective is to climb Dúchruach. Leave the Visitor Centre and follow the tarmac road up towards the Abbey. Turn left along another

narrow tarmac road, passing a gate beside a monkey puzzle
tree, to reach the staff car park on the western side of the
building. A sign indicates 'Path to Statue' and a flight of steps
leads up to a small gate. Go through the gate and continue up
another flight of steps.

*The rugged, wooded, steep-
sided Dúchruach rises above
Kylemore Abbey, Kylemore
Lough and Kylemore Pass.*

**b** The path zig-zags uphill, sometimes on steps and
sometimes on rugged stones, but it is always clear and
obvious. The steep, well-wooded slope includes beech, oak,
birch, holly and masses of rhododendron. A metal rail runs
alongside the path at one point, and small metal crosses
stand beside the path. Emerging from the trees, the path
climbs to a white statue, with arms outstretched, embracing
the Kylemore estate and the Connemara National Park. This
is a fine viewpoint, and is about as far as many casual walkers
are prepared to venture. Feral goats may be spotted in the
woods or on the slopes of Dúchruach.

Seen from the slopes of Maolan, Kylemore Abbey and its woodlands grace the lower slopes of Dúchruach.

## B  Birds of Prey

The area around Kylemore offers perhaps the best opportunity to see the full range of birds of prey in Connemara. The little merlin is fairly common, hunting between the coast and lower areas of bog. The kestrel is more easily identified because of its singular hunting method, by hovering mostly over open ground, though it will sometimes perch on a tree to scan an area. The sparrowhawk prefers wooded areas, and more particularly deciduous woods, so Kylemore is one of its haunts. The peregrine is the largest bird of prey in Ireland and it will hunt over both the glens and the higher mountains. It is most likely to be spotted after uttering a piercing scream in flight. The mountains remain largely the preserve of the raven, which will readily mob even the peregrine for approaching its terrain.

c  The path continues gradually uphill and across the steep slopes of Dúchruach. At times the path is broad and grassy, but sometimes it is narrow and stony, or even lost in areas of

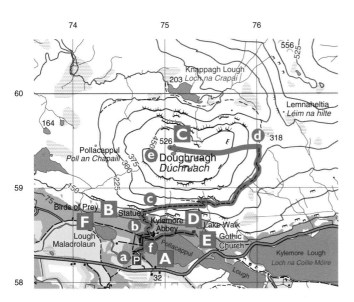

bog. It can generally be distinguished by its obvious, engineered surface and kerbstones. A few boulders have been marked with a dot of red paint where the path is vague. Note the rugged upper slopes of Dúchruach, the buttresses, gullies and huge boulders. The underlying rock is an ancient, dark and rough textured gabbro, which is unusual in Ireland. Follow the path around the slopes, and certainly no further than a broad and boggy gap.

**d**  When the ground rising steeply to the left appears somewhat less rugged and a little more grassy, pick a course uphill. Grass and short heather lead towards low outcrops of rock and embedded boulders, becoming rather more rugged towards the top. The broad top of Dúchruach is a confusing place in mist, being composed of hummocky outcrops of rock, hollows filled with small lakes, with sheep paths that appear to head nowhere. The main summit cairn is easily identified on a clear day, being higher than any contenders and accompanied by a couple of rusting iron fenceposts.

### C  Dúchruach 751595
Dúchruach is Anglicised as Doughruagh and means Black Stack. It rises to 1736ft (526m) and offers a fine view. Mweelrea can be seen rising over Maolchnoc, with Binn Gorm and the Devilsmother seen at the head of Killary Harbour. Leenane Hill

A popular view of Kylemore Abbey seen across a reedy area of the lough from a point near the Visitor Centre.

and the Maum Turk Mountains give way to views of the Twelve Bens. Maolan, Cnoc Breac and Diamond Hill are seen in all their glory rising south of Kylemore. Tully Mountain and distant Inis Tuirc are seen, along with sizeable stretches of coastline.

**e** A descent could be made directly southwards, but this would need great care as the buttresses and gullies are unstable and need careful handling. It is much preferable to retrace steps faithfully all the way to Kylemore Abbey. Any other line turns this moderate hill walk into quite a difficult walk. It is best to return to the Abbey in any case, as there is so much more still to be seen there.

## D   The Lake Walk 747585

Running along the shore of Kylemore Lough, the Lake Walk includes an informative tree trail with 22 stops, a chance to visit the Gothic Church, as well as the Mausoleum containing Margaret, Mitchell and John Henry. The route is short, easy and entirely on a tarmac path. The woodlands include native Irish and introduced species, nearly all planted on the orders of Mitchell Henry. A guide to the trail, obtainable from the Visitor Centre, helps with identification. The trees are given their common English names, scientific Latin names, and in the case of native species, their Irish names too. Of particular note is the Irish Yew, which in legend is descended from a yew planted at Newry by St. Patrick, but which was actually a freak of nature found in 1740 by George Willis on the slopes of Cuilcagh in Co Fermanagh. All Irish Yews worldwide are descended from cuttings taken from the original tree. By coincidence, Kylemore as a placename is derived from An Choill Mhóir, which means The Big Wood. Birds to spot include the blue/great/coal/long-tailed tit, chaffinch and cuckoo.

**f**   The route description is simple. In between the Visitor Centre and the Abbey, the Lake Walk is signposted along a level tarmac path. This has clipped hedges of rhododendron at first, then runs close to the shores of the lake, with a spur leading to the Gothic Church towards the end. The Mausoleum lies a short way beyond the Gothic Church. Again, simply retrace steps afterwards to return to the visitor centre and car park.

## E   The Gothic Church 753585

This architectural gem is neatly tucked away in the woods at the foot of Dúchruach. It was built by Mitchell Henry in memory of his wife Margaret, who died in 1874. The construction spanned the years 1877 to 1881. Exquisite attention to detail has resulted in this little building being called a 'cathedral in miniature' and its form incorporates elements from the great English cathedrals. Marble pillars inside come from all four provinces of Ireland. The exterior is of well-dressed limestone containing an abundance of fossils; productids, crinoids and corals. The roofspace of the church is inhabited by a colony of Natterer's bats. The colony dwindled in size during recent restoration work, but now seems to be well on the way to recovery following completion of the work in 1994.

### F   Projects at Kylemore

Quite apart from their spiritual pursuits, running a boarding school and catering for tourists, the Benedictine nuns of Kylemore have a number of interesting projects in various stages of development. They produce foodstuffs and manage a traditional farm, and the Victorian walled gardens have been restored. There is also a woodland project in progress, with specific conservation aims. Visitors might like to make their mark on the area by sponsoring the planting of a tree before leaving. The site also includes a restaurant, craft shop and pottery.

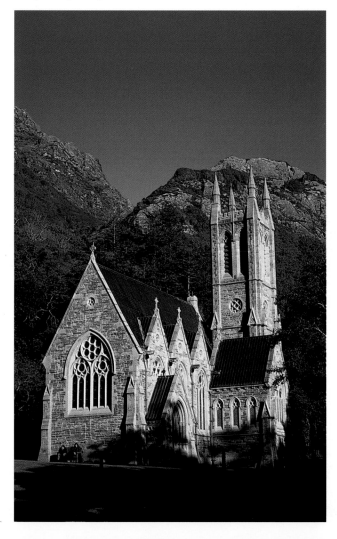

The Gothic Church incorporates features from some of the great English cathedrals. It was built in the years 1877–81.

# CREERAGH CHURCH AND MAOLCHNOC

**M**aolchnoc is the highest summit in the range of hills situated between the Twelve Bens and Killary Harbour. A walk over Maolchnoc can be accomplished in a horseshoe route based on Creeragh and its strikingly modern church. There are fine and extensive views from the summit. Both the ascent and descent are on well-graded grassy ridges which are mostly dry underfoot, though there is an extensive area of squelchy bog to be crossed at the foot of the hills.

## A    Creeragh Church 799593

There are actually two churches at Creeragh, on a bleak and barren stretch of the main N59 road between Kylemore and Leenane. One church is almost completely surrounded by trees, while the other is a remarkable modern structure rising from an open stretch of bogland. The old church was built by Mitchell Henry of Kylemore in 1870. He built it for his brother Alex, who had converted to Catholicism and become a Jesuit priest. The more modern church, dedicated to Our Lady of the Wayside, was built in 1968. The award-winning design was by the architect Leo Mansfield. It has been described as a

**START/FINISH:**
At Creeragh Church, a modern and unusually designed church on the main N59 road between Leenane and Kylemore.

**DISTANCE:** 6 miles (9.5km).

**APPROXIMATE TIME:**
3½ hours.

**HIGHEST POINT:**
1973ft (598m) on the summit of Maolchnoc.

**MAPS:** Harveys Superwalker Connemara; OS Sheet 37.

**REFRESHMENTS:**
None on the route. The Pass Inn Hotel is down the main N59 road in the direction of Kylemore.

**ADVICE:**
A fairly straightforward hill walk. There are no paths, but in clear weather there should be no problem with navigation. The lower slopes are usually wet and boggy.

From the Kylemore River in the Inagh Valley, both of Maolchnoc's ridges can be observed.

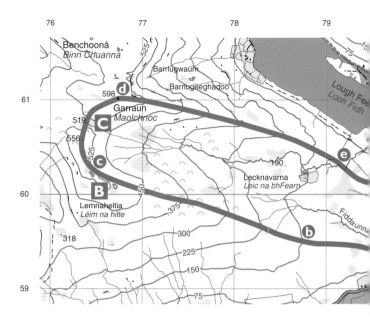

'pegged-down tent on the windswept Connemara Plain'. There is a striking red and blue window by Phyllis Burke, simple metalwork Stations of the Cross and plain Connemara Marble holy water stoups. The exposed and slightly elevated situation affords fine views of the Maum Turk Mountains, the Inagh Valley and the Twelve Bens.

**a** There is a small car park in front of Creeragh Church, but please do not use it if the church is likely to be in use. There are other small roadside spaces available in the direction of Leenane. Follow the road away from the church in the direction of Leenane to locate a gravel bank spanning a deep roadside drainage ditch. Turn left to cross the ditch, then continue across the squelchy bog, drifting to the left towards Maolchnoc. The near level bog is grassy and usually wet underfoot. There is a small stream to cross, little humps of rock to pass and a couple of rhododendron shrubs to spot. Take care as there are some areas of quaking bog. Note the growth of purple moor grass, bog asphodel and bog myrtle.

**b** The ground begins to rise and the boggy slope becomes drier underfoot. There are only a few little outcrops of rock and the climb is fairly gentle. The slope steepens a little with

80          81

Bunowen
Bun Abhann
ınroe
48
Lake
Dwelling
Bog Pine
D Owenduff
Bridge
g 63
Lough
Nacarrigeen
a
A
Creeragh
Church

upward progress and there are patches of decaying blanket bog which sometimes need to be side-stepped. Towards the top there is a steeper slope of short grass and moss, ending with a few rocky slabs and a cairn at 1717ft (522m). The cairn is not on the true summit, but it does mark an especially fine view across Kylemore Lough to the Twelve Bens. This area is known as Léim na hEltia.

**B   Léim na hEltia**
Anglicised as Lemnaheltia, Léim na hEltia translates as the Leap of the Doe. It is said that the warrior Fionn Mac Cumhail's faithful hound Bran fell from this spot while chasing a doe during the heat of a hunt. The dog fell all the way down to the lough below. Tales of Fionn Mac Cumhail and the warrior caste of the Fianna are thought to have originated in the 3rd Century AD, passed on from generation to generation in an oral tradition before being compiled in writing by historians and folklorists.

c   Continue along the broad crest of the hill, passing a pool of water and a rocky outcrop. There is a line of old fenceposts on the boggy summit, but these don't lead in any useful direction, so disregard them. Head to the right to cross a gap

Dhubh, Binn Bhán, Binn Bhraoin, Binn Fhraoigh, Binn Leitrí, Meacanach, Binn Bhreac, An Chailleach, Cnoc Breac and Cregg Hill. Nearby Dúchruach and Diamond Hill give way to Tully Mountain and islands such as Inis Bó Finne, Inis Tuirc, Achill and Clare Island. Back on the mainland are Corraun Hill and parts of the Nephin Beg Range.

**d** The descent is eastwards from the summit of Maolchnoc. The ridge is steep, falling in distinct steps with superb views straight down to the left overlooking Loch Fidh. There are some rocky outcrops, but nothing which will bar progress. Some of the outcrops are of an extremely coarse and steeply tilted bouldery conglomerate. The slope is mostly grassy and mossy, with some coarse woodrush also growing in patches. Most of the way the ground is firm and dry, though there are a few boggy patches. There are masses of rhododendron growing in the shallow valley off to the right, along with a few little conifers.

**e** When the river in the valley swings left and cuts across the foot of the ridge, cross over to the other side. The riverbanks are clothed in rhododendron scrub, but there is a gap where the river makes a pronounced bend. Continue across a broad rise of boggy ground beyond. There is a fence off to the left. Follow this fence to a corner, then head down towards a track which is in view below. Notice the sphagnum moss, bog myrtle and bog cotton in the boggy surroundings.

**f** Turn right to follow the track across the boggy slope near the head of Loch Fidh. There are some turf cuttings just before the main N59 road is reached. Looking to the right in these cuttings, there are some good exposed examples of bog pine roots.

### D  Bog Pine 803596
Prominent stumps of bog pine have been exposed by turf cutting, near the junction of the farm track and the main road. Following a climatic change in the Bronze Age, conditions favoured the growth of blanket bog. Another shift in the climate appears to have dried the bog sufficiently for it to be invaded by Scots Pine. However, with wetter conditions again becoming established, the inexorable growth of the bog killed the trees. The tree trunks also rarely survived as they were valuable, dug up for fuel use and traditionally exported to Galway via the Maam Valley and the Corrib. Some imaginative artists have dried and carved remaining wood into exquisite ornaments.

of worn blanket bog and stony patches, then climb up a grassy slope and pass a broken outcrop of rock to reach a large summit cairn on top of Maolchnoc.

A view of the Maum Turk Mountains from a point close to the start at Creeragh Church.

### C   Maolchnoc 767610

The Ordnance Survey names this summit as Garraun, but locally it is known as Maolchnoc, meaning the Bald Hill. The summit cairn stands at 1973ft (598m) and the view is quite extensive. Look for Mweelrea across the fjord-like Killary Harbour, then take in the Sheeffry Hills, Binn Gorm, Mám Trasna, Devilsmother and Leenane Hill. The Maum Turk Mountains include Binn Bhán, Binn Bhriocáin, Binn Idir an Dá Log, Binn Mhór and Leic Aimhréidh. Solitary Cnoc Lios Uachtair sits at the end of the Inagh Valley. The Twelve Bens feature Binn Charrach, Binn an Choire Bhig, Binn Chorr, Binn

An extensive network of bog pine roots have been exposed by turf-cutting towards the end of the walk.

**g** Turn right to follow the main road. There are some trees growing to the right: alder, holly, sycamore, as well as some rhododendrons. where the ruins of the old Creeragh Church are hidden. There is a little house alongside, with hedgerows of alder and fuschia being passed before an open stretch of road continues across the bog. Creeragh Church is seen just ahead, marking the conclusion of the walk.

# LETTERGESH AND MAOLCHNOC

**M**aolchnoc is the highest of a range of hills situated between the Twelve Bens and Killary Harbour sometimes called the Northern Bens. A walk over Maolchnoc can be accomplished in a rugged horseshoe route based on the straggly village of Lettergesh. There are fine and extensive views from the summit. Both the ascent and descent are on rugged ridges which are often quite firm underfoot, though there are some boggy patches. An old bog road is followed down from the hills.

## A Lettergesh 749634

Lettergesh, is a small, straggly village on a minor road between Letterfrack and the mouth of Killary Harbour. It has a Post Office and foodstore, as well as a caravan and camp site. Access is achieved in a roundabout way by following narrow minor roads, starting from the Killary Harbour road or from Letterfrack on the main N59 road.

**a** Start at King's Foodstore in Lettergesh, which also houses the Post Office. It is situated at the head of a reedy inlet from the sea at the mouth of the Culfin River. Facing the store, there is a narrow tarmac road to the right, and this should be followed first. It is flanked by unruly hedgerows of fuchsia,

**START/FINISH:**
At King's Foodstore and Post Office in the straggly village of Lettergesh. Anyone using the Connemara Caravan Park and Camp Site could start at that point.

**DISTANCE:** 6 miles (9.5km).

**APPROXIMATE TIME:**
3½ hours.

**HIGHEST POINT:**
1973ft (598m) on the summit of Maolchnoc.

**MAPS:** Harveys Superwalker Connemara; OS Sheet 37.

**REFRESHMENTS:**
None actually on the route, though there is King's Foodstore and the small shop at the Connemara Caravan Park and Camp Site.

**ADVICE:**
The route is easier to follow in a clockwise direction. The ascent is steep and rugged, and the walk from summit to summit needs care in mist. The descent is simple provided that the course of the old bog road is followed through the lower fields.

Seen from near Dawros Bridge, Maolchnoc's western ridges are apparent to the left of the darker Dúchruach.

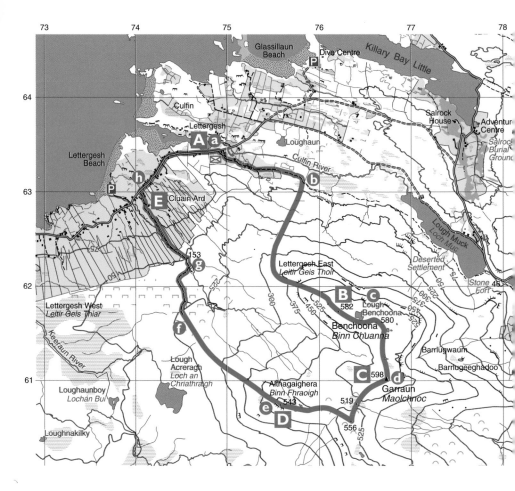

willow and bramble. After passing a few houses, the end of the tarmac is reached. On the left are a couple of gates leading through a sheepfold, followed by a broad, rugged, grassy track. There is another gateway, then a right turn leads to a fence, which is crossed to reach the open mountainside beyond.

**b** Climb uphill, picking a way on grassy areas between rock outcrops. There is a little valley to cross behind the first rise, then there is a steeper, rougher climb up the slopes of Binn Chuanna. There is a little bracken on the slope at first, but the higher parts feature grass and heather. When the crest of a broad ridge is reached, turn left to face another steep and

Binn Fhraoigh's crest features a series of shapely peaks, formed from a coarse, bouldery conglomerate.

rocky slope. Pick any way uphill which seems to offer the least resistance; the slope is grassier to the left, though there are rock outcrops in all directions. St. Patrick's cabbage is noticeable here. The gradient eases to reveal a summit area of hummocky, rocky, heathery ground with small pools of water. There is a large cairn reached on an outcrop, but there is another cairn further away which is slightly higher. In mist the top of Binn Chuanna is a potentially confusing place.

### B   Binn Chuanna 763617
Anglicised as Benchoona, Binn Chuanna is steep, rough and rocky on most sides and rises to 1919ft (581m). There are good views towards the mouth of Killary Harbour.

c   Walking across the broad and hummocky crest of Binn Chuanna involves passing the little Loch Binn Chuanna, then later turning right to cross a gap occupied by another small

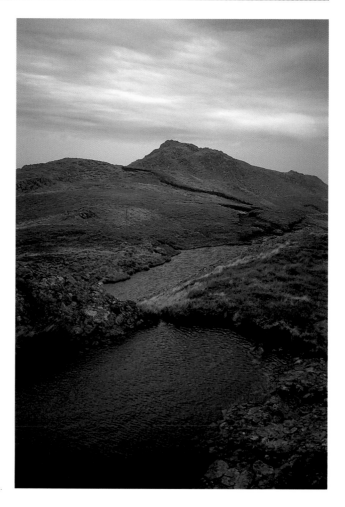

Peaks and hollows occur along the crest of Binn Fhraoigh. The summit lies beyond a small pool.

pool and a spiky outcrop of rock. There is a short, steep, grassy climb to the summit cairn on Maolchnoc.

### C  Maolchnoc 767610

The Ordnance Survey names this summit as Garraun, but locally it is known as Maolchnoc, meaning the Bald Hill. The summit cairn stands at 1973ft (598m) and the view is quite extensive. Look for Mweelrea across the fjord-like Killary Harbour, then take in the Sheeffry Hills, Binn Gorm, Mám Trasna, Devilsmother and Leenane Hill. The Maum Turk Mountains include Binn Bhán, Binn Bhriocáin, Binn Idir an Dá Log, Binn Mhór and Leic Aimhréidh. Solitary Cnoc Lios Uachtair sits at the end of the Inagh Valley. The Twelve Bens feature Binn Charrach, Binn an Choire Bhig, Binn Chorr, Binn Dhubh, Binn Bhán, Binn Bhraoin, Binn Fhraoigh, Binn Leitrí, Meacanach, Binn Bhreac, An Chailleach, Cnoc Breac and Cregg Hill. Nearby Dúchruach and Diamond Hill give way to Tully Mountain and islands such as Inis Bó Finne, Inis Tuirc, Achill and Clare Island. Back on the mainland are Corraun Hill and parts of the Nephin Beg Range.

d  Turn right on Maolchnoc to descend south-westwards to a boggy, stony gap, passing a broken rock outcrop on the way. The next grassy summit bears a small cairn, but it is also possible to walk westwards across the slope to approach the pinnacled summit of Binn Fhraoigh more directly. A series of jagged peaks turn out to be composed of a coarse, bouldery conglomerate. Walk over as many, or as few of them as are required. A few old wooden fenceposts will be noticed. The highest point bears no cairn.

### D  Binn Fhraoigh 756607

The Ordnance Survey name this peak as Altnagaighera, but also admit that in Irish it is Binn Fhraoigh, meaning the Heather Peak. The bouldery conglomerate rock weathers in a way which allows its rounded boulders to fall from outcrops, forming a sort of scree of rounded pebbles, which looks unusual in a mountain setting and seems more appropriate to a coastal storm beach! The conglomerate is very steeply tilted, attesting to considerable earth movements since it was first laid in horizontal beds. The highest point rises to 1791ft (543m) and bears no cairn or other marker.

e  Walk down the steep ridge from the summit. If this ridge is followed all the way down, then beware of a series of rocksteps which appear quite suddenly. Alternatively, drop down a steep, grassy slope to the left of the ridge and walk down a valley, looking up and down to spot cliffs, caves and huge boulders which have become detached from the main bed of the conglomerate. The slope levels out and gives way to a rugged heather moorland on decaying blanket bog.

f  Aim to reach the end of an old bog road on the moorland. This is easier to distinguish from a height, than at close quarters. There is only a vague grassy track, heathery and rushy in places, leading down from the moorland. The line becomes clearer when a stream is approached, crossing a concrete bridge over a rocky gorge. This is the perfect setting for rowan, holly, oak, St. Patrick's cabbage, ferns and bramble.

**g** The gorge is fenced and the track runs alongside it down towards the coast. The track later narrows as it passes through an area of gorse, then is mostly hemmed in between low drystone walls as it continues downhill. The track is clear all the way down, though there are a couple of low fences which need to be crossed. At the bottom, a gate gives way to a stony track. Turn right to follow this away from a couple of houses to reach the minor road which runs through Lettergesh.

### E   Cluain Ard 743628

Standing on a brow above the road at Lettergesh and requiring another short ascent just as the road is reached, is a poorly-preserved stone cashel or stone fort at Cluain Ard, reused as a cattle pound. This would have been occupied by an extended family group, who would be able to retreat inside the structure during times of local raids. It is positioned to allow a good view of approaches both from the coast and from the hills above.

**h** Turn right and follow the road across a bridge. Pass the entrance to the Connemara Caravan Park and Camp Site, which has a small shop and continue along the road, passing hedgerows of fuchsia and brambles, to return to King's Foodstore.

A huge detached boulder lies embedded in a moorland at the foot of a cliff on Binn Fhraoigh.

# BINN MHÓR, LOCH MUC AND LOCH FIDH

Couched between Killary Harbour and Loch Fidh, Binn Mhór is a small hill with a mighty outlook. Even though it is hemmed in by the higher mountains of Mweelrea and Maolchnoc, views are quite extensive. A walk over Binn Mhór is relatively easy, taking in a rugged, pathless ridge of grassy bog and rocky outcrops. A circuit can be created by walking along the road beside Loch Fidh. In fact, there is an optional short circular walk around Loch Muc which can be used to extend the distance with ease.

**START/FINISH:**
On the minor road running from the main N59 road towards Killary Harbour, at a point in between the main road and Loch Fidh.

**DISTANCE:** 8 miles (13km).

**APPROXIMATE TIME:** 4 hours.

**HIGHEST POINT:** 1105ft (333m) on the summit of Binn Mhór.

**MAPS:** Harveys Superwalker Connemara; OS Sheet 37.

**REFRESHMENTS:** None on the route. The Pass Inn Hotel lies along the main road at Kylemore and other places offering food and drink can be found in the opposite direction at Leenane.

**ADVICE:** The walk is fairly easy in good weather, though there are some boggy patches and rocky areas which need to be outflanked.

Using the circular stone cashel as a viewpoint, a gap in the mountains offers a peep towards Loch Fidh.

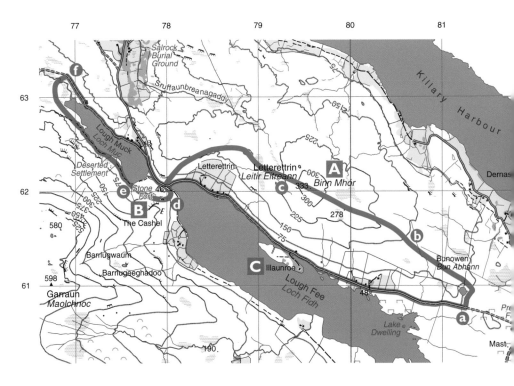

**a** The start of this walk is on a minor road leading to Killary Harbour from the main N59 road. The walk could be started from the occasional bus service on the main road, though if a car is driven down the road it can be parked in any one of the small roadside spaces. Start the walk by following the first fence off to the right, which leads over a boggy rise to a small pool of water. Pass the pool, turn left and step over a fence. A fairly level area of bog leads towards a small stream which features a drystone embankment on one side. Note the purple moor grass and bog myrtle growing well in this area.

**b** Start climbing along the broad crest of Binn Mhór. The ground is grassy, with rock outcrops which are easily side-stepped. There is a significant little rocky gap along the crest, which is best passed by keeping to the left. The rest of the ascent is fairly straightforward, though there is no trodden path on the way to the large summit cairn.

### A Binn Mhór 796620
Binn Mhór means the Big Peak, yet the summit cairn stands

at an altitude of only 1105ft (333m). The view, however, is remarkably extensive. Starting from Mweelrea, the vista includes the Sheeffry Hills, Binn Gorm and Devilsmother. The Maum Turk Mountains include Leenane Hill, Cnoc an Doirín, Binn Bhán and Binn Bhriocáin. Cnoc Lios Uachtair sits at the end of the Inagh Valley. The Twelve Bens feature Binn an Choire Bhig, Binn Chorr, Binn Dhubh, Binn Bhán, Binn Fhraoigh, Meacanach, Binn Bhreac, An Chailleach and Cnoc Breac. Maolchnoc and Binn Chuanna rise closer to hand across Loch Fidh. Looking out to sea reveals Inis Tuirc, Clare Island and Achill. Binn Mhór is flanked on its northern side by the long, fjord-like sea inlet of Killary Harbour.

Looking across Loch Muc, there is a little chapel beside a road, while the mountain of Mweelrea towers above it.

Crossing a footbridge over the river which flows from Loch Muc. The bridge leads to a series of small turf cuttings.

**c**  Walk further along the crest of Binn Mhór, away from the cairn then descend a grassy slope, stepping around any little rocky outcrops. Descend steeply towards a gap which may be boggy, then climb uphill, keeping to the left side of the next rise. A descent can be made diagonally leftwards down to an unfenced stretch of road between Loch Fidh and Loch Muc.

**d**  An optional walk around Loch Muc, which translates as the Pig Lake, can be enjoyed by following a gravel track on the other side of the road. This leads through a gate, where a sharp right turn can be made alongside a fence. When another fence has been crossed at a junction, climb steeply uphill for a short distance to discover a circular stone cashel overlooking Loch Muc.

**B  The Cashel 779619**
The circular stone-walled cashel, or small fort, is now in a tumbled state and invaded by rushes. It occupies a strategic position on a steep-sided shoulder, with even steeper ground rising above it to Binn Chuanna. The occupants would have been able to observe anyone on the lower ground approaching from either Loch Fidh or Loch Muc. Cashels of this type were usually inhabited by extended family groups and were quite common from the Iron Age to early Christian times.

**e**  Continue along the grassy shore of Loch Muc, where there are some vague paths and the remains of a 19th-Century deserted settlement with extensive cultivation ridges. There is a fine view back from the foot of Loch Muc, through the valley to the conical form of Binn Bhriocáin in the Maum Turk Mountains. Follow the river flowing out of Loch Muc, then cross a wooden footbridge to reach the road once again.

f   Turn right along the road, passing the little white chapel and continuing along the shore of Loch Muc. A couple of houses are passed where the hillside is quite well wooded with scots pine, sycamore, birch, rhododendron, fuchsia and gorse. The road continues through a gap between Binn Mhór and Binn Chuanna, to run alongside Loch Fidh. The road runs close to the shoreline, passing a couple of farms and houses on the rugged slopes of Binn Mhór. There is the wooded promontory of Illaunroe to the right, then the road gradually drifts away from the shore of the lough to return to the starting point.

### C   Illaunroe 794613
Illaunroe is the Anglicised version of Oileán Rua, or the Red Island. It is a wooded promontory which breaks the otherwise clear lines of Loch Fidh. A lodge was built out on the point in 1853 as a summer residence for Dr William Wilde, one of Ireland's foremost 19th-Century doctors and antiquarians. His son, the playwright Oscar Wilde, stayed at the house and fished in Loch Fidh in the years 1876–8.

A view of Binn Mhór's rugged slopes seen rising above small farmsteads towards the end of the walk.

# KILLARY HARBOUR COASTAL WALK

## START:
On the main N59 road at its junction with the minor road to Bunowen. Parking can be difficult and is limited to small spaces beside the road and disused quarry.

## FINISH:
Killary Harbour Youth Hostel, where parking is limited to a small area between the Youth Hostel and the tiny harbour.

## DISTANCE: 5 miles (8km).

## APPROXIMATE TIME:
2 hours.

## HIGHEST POINT:
200ft (60m) at the start on the main road.

## MAPS: Harveys Superwalker Connemara; OS Sheet 37.

## REFRESHMENTS:
None on the route, or closer than Leenane or Kylemore on the main N59 road.

## ADVICE:
An easy coastal walk on good surfaces. Ideal for reaching the Youth Hostel, but also a good choice on a day of poor weather.

The coastal path on the south side of Killary Harbour offers one of the best coastal walks in Connemara. There is a minor road leading to the coast at Bunowen, then a series of clear tracks and paths can be linked to reach Rosroe. The walk described here is linear and is essentially easy. It could be used even by heavily laden backpackers wishing to reach the Killary Harbour Youth Hostel from the bus services on the main road. The 'harbour' is actually a fjord-like sea inlet, dominated by the mountain of Mweelrea.

**a** Start on the main N59 road where an unsignposted, unenclosed minor road runs down to Bunowen. The only indicator for this road is a boulder marked 'Bunowen' and 'Bun Abhann' which means the Foot of the River. Follow the road downhill past turf cuttings where the stumps of bog pine are exposed.

## A  Bog Pine 521607
Prominent stumps of bog pine have been exposed by turf cutting near the junction of the Bunowen road and the main road. Following a climatic change in the Bronze Age, conditions favoured the growth of blanket bog. Another shift in the climate appears to have dried the bog sufficiently for it to be invaded by Scots Pine. However, with wetter conditions again becoming established, the inexorable growth of the bog killed the trees. The boles will have rotted and been toppled, but the roots have been very well preserved in the bog. While bog pine has sometimes been harvested and dried for fuel, these days it is simply discarded. Some imaginative artists have dried and carved the wood into exquisite ornaments.

**b** The road has a patchy surface and overlooks a wooded valley where a river rushes towards Killary Harbour. Here, you are likely to see foxglove, bracken, oak, holly and ash; ahead, the vast bulk of Mweelrea is seen rising above the waters of Killary Harbour. Pass a couple of houses and farm buildings, then go through a gate on a gentle rise in the road.

**c** The tarmac road gives way to a broad and firm gravel track, which runs gently downhill across a rugged moorland slope. A small stand of conifers is passed, and there is a house just beyond the trees. Also note the boathouse building

An overburdened signpost stands by the road on a barren stretch of bogland near the start of the walk.

and slipway down to the right of the track: these are associated with the mussel fisheries in Killary Harbour.

## B Killary Harbour

The long sea inlet of Killary Harbour is a true fjord, being long and narrow, bounded by mountains, and deeper along its length than at its mouth. Indeed, its mouth is almost blocked by the island of Inis Bearna. The inlet was scoured by the force of several Connemara glaciers in the Ice Age. The rafts and barrels which disfigure the surface of the water are used to breed salmon and mussels, a valuable indigenous export. The track which has been followed so far has been improved

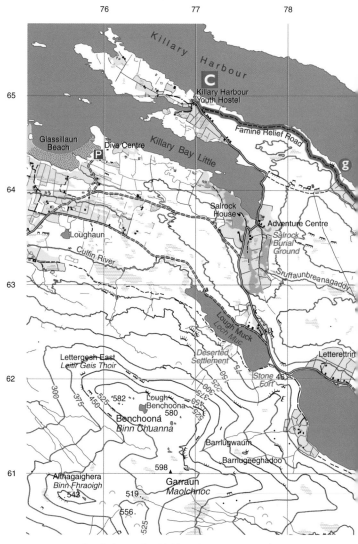

to service the fishery. In 1903 a British naval fleet dropped anchor in Killary Harbour, so that King Edward VII and Queen Alexandra could take a sightseeing tour of Connemara. This tour included stops at nearby Kylemore and Leenane. Killary Harbour is the northernmost boundary of Connemara, while Mweelrea, rising above the opposite shore in Co. Mayo, is the highest mountain in the Province of Connacht.

**d** Cross a stile beside a gate and continue along the track. The way ahead is unenclosed, though there are some trees

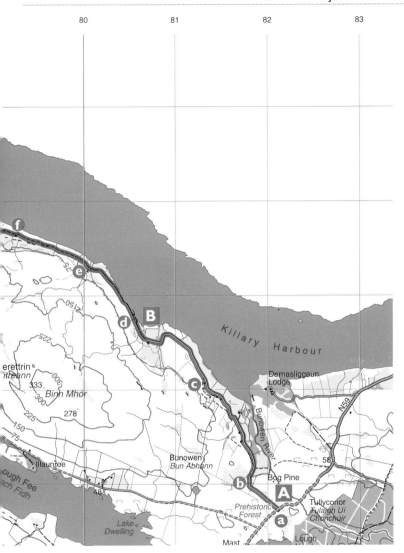

between the track and the sea. Oak, birch, holly, rowan, hazel and hawthorn are visble and, from time to time, a school of dolphins. Cross another stile beside a gate, and immediately cross a concrete slab bridge where a waterfall tumbles into Killary Harbour from the slopes of Binn Mhór.

**e** The track is becoming more and more grassy, maybe even muddy when wet, and now has the low ruins of a drystone wall to the seaward side. This is an inviting habitat for wrens and wheatears. Keep following the track, then go through a gate

A small waterfall tumbles down the slopes of Binn Mhór, passing beneath the track to enter Killary Harbour.

in a drystone wall. The track continues with a drystone wall and fence on the seaward side, then passes a small cottage, at Foher, which has a clump of rhododendrons alongside. Another small cottage can be seen further away, uphill from the track. There are also a handful of roofless ruins and a series of 'lazy beds' where potatoes were once grown. The area shows signs of depopulation following the Great Famine.

**f** Keep walking along the grassy track, passing through a small iron gate in a wall, and continuing to a stile over the next wall. The track shows distinct signs of engineering, and there is a short, steep section where it climbs across an inclined cliff face. The rest of the old track is unfenced, crossing a rugged slope above Killary Harbour. Some parts are broad and grassy, while other parts are very stony. Some stretches feature only a narrow path, or even cut across bare slabs of rock.

**g** Look out for ferns, liverworts and St. Patrick's cabbage where there are damp and dark crevices in the rocks. On the moorland slopes, tormentil grows, with sundew and butterwort on the boggy patches. Follow the coastal path

A cottage at Foher is passed by the coastal track in an area showing signs of depopulation in the Great Famine.

Killary Harbour Youth Hostel stands alongside The tiny harbour at Rosroe at the end of the walk.

until it is diverted away from the sea by a drystone wall. The grassy track is leads to a cottage and a minor road. Turn right to follow the road to Killary Harbour Youth Hostel at Rosroe.

### C  Killary Harbour Youth Hostel 769650
This building was formerly called Rosroe Cottage. A plaque affixed to the wall records 'Bord Fáilte Éireann. Ludwig Wittgenstein, 1889–1951, Philosopher, lived and worked here April 1948–Oct 1948.' The tiny harbour beside the hostel usually features lobster post and traditional fishing boats, the currach. There is no further access towards the nearby Killary Salmon Fishery. Anyone not staying in the hostel will either need to arrange to be collected at this point, or retrace steps back along the shore to return to the main road.

# KILLARY HARBOUR AND SALROCK PASS

There is a fine, easy walk available between the two sea inlets of Killary Harbour and Little Killary. The route uses a minor road, tracks and paths, nearly always with good coastal and mountain views. The route description is based on Killary Harbour Youth Hostel, taking in a walk alongside Little Killary before crossing over to the lower reaches of Killary Harbour itself. The short circular walk is suitable for use in most weathers, but in fine weather the scenery can be astounding for such a short and easy walk.

**START/FINISH:**
At Killary Harbour Youth Hostel, where a small amount of parking is available beside the tiny harbour.

**DISTANCE:** 3 miles (5km).

**APPROXIMATE TIME:**
2.5 hours.

**HIGHEST POINT:**
425ft (130m) on the top of the Salrock Pass.

**MAPS:** Harveys Superwalker Connemara; OS Sheet 37.

**REFRESHMENTS:**
None on the route. It is necessary to drive well away from Killary Harbour towards Leenane, Kylemore or Tully Cross.

**ADVICE:**
This short, easy walk is suitable for use in any weather. In heavy rain the water cascades down the steep slopes of Mweelrea. The scenery is so good, in such short compass, that it really should be sampled.

A small boat is moored on the shore of Little Killary close to where the route crosses the Salrock Pass.

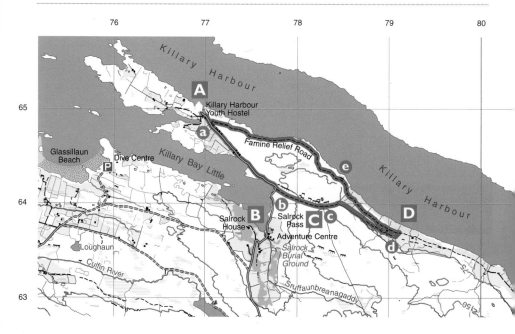

### A   Killary Harbour Youth Hostel 769650

The cottage beside the tiny harbour at Rosroe has been converted and extended by An Oige as a Youth Hostel. A plaque fixed to the wall reads: 'Bord Fáilte Éireann. Ludwig Wittgenstein, 1889–1951, Philosopher, Lived and Worked Here April 1948 – Oct 1948.' The harbour usually features lobster pots and traditional round-bottomed Connemara Currach, while the Killary Salmon Fishery can be seen further westwards.

The storm-tossed Killary Harbour is a glacial fjord, flanked on both sides by rugged mountain slopes.

A rocky point projects into Killary Harbour at Rosroe. The steep slopes of Mweelrea rise across the water.

a   Follow the road inland from the Youth Hostel and harbour, passing a few little cottages, including a row of fishermen's cottages at the foot of a cliff. The road continues alongside the smaller sea inlet of Little Killary, passing a few gnarled oaks. The road rises and offers a fine view towards the head of Little Killary, where small boats are usually moored. When the road drops, look out for a little gate on the left.

## B   Salrock House 775637

Looking across the waters of Little Killary, Salrock House can be seen in wooded surroundings. The local landlords were the Thompsons, who were given the land around Salrock by Cromwell in the 17th Century. In the 19th Century, somewhat before other landlords began similar schemes, tenants were evicted from their farms and houses to clear the land for sheep grazing.

**b**  Go through the gate and cross a small stream. Follow a track uphill, with a line of telegraph poles to the right and heaps of huge boulders to the left. The track leads to the top of the rugged Salrock Pass.

### C  Salrock Pass 783640

The rugged, bouldery gap of Salrock Pass is said to have been created when the Devil tried to drag the St. Roc over the hills with a chain. Geologists, however, state that the pass lies along the line of an excavated fault in the bedrock. It is said that smugglers landing contraband at Little Killary were in the habit of moving their goods over the Salrock Pass to Foher and so along the shore of Killary Harbour to progress further inland. There are a series of small stone monuments which were used as resting places for coffins being brought from the village of Foher to the early monastic site and graveyard at Salrock.

**c**  The path crosses a rugged gap and descends with a wall and fence to the right – this is wet, boggy and slippery in places. The telegraph poles are now on the left. The path downhill can be steep, stony and muddy. Cross a fence on the right at the corner of a wall, then go through a little iron gate. Turn right to follow a grassy path beside the wall, gradually drifting downhill to pass a cottage at Foher. Note the handful of ruined buildings on the slope, the old enclosures, remains of a once-thriving 19th-Century baile (hamlet) and, of course, the long sea inlet of Killary Harbour.

### D  Killary Harbour

The long sea inlet of Killary Harbour is a true fjord, being long and narrow, bounded by mountains, and deeper along its length than at its mouth. Indeed, its mouth is almost blocked by the island of Inis Bearna. The inlet was scoured by several combined Connemara glaciers in the Ice Age. The rafts and barrels which disfigure the surface of the water are used to hold salmon cages and mussel beds in place along the line of the sheltered inlet. The track which has been followed so far has been improved to service the fishery. In 1903 a British naval fleet dropped anchor in Killary Harbour, allowing King Edward VII and Queen Alexandra to take a sightseeing tour of Connemara. This tour included stops at nearby Kylemore and Leenane. Killary Harbour is the northernmost boundary of Connemara, while Mweelrea, rising above the opposite shore, is the highest mountain in the Province of Connacht.

**d**  Drop down onto a lower grassy track and turn left,

walking alongside a drystone wall. There are gaps in other drystone walls, then there is a wall-stile to cross. The track is well engineered and has a stone banking to the right and a low cliff to the left. There is a short climb uphill, then the track is gently undulating. Look in the damp cracks and crevices in the cliff to spot a range of plants: St. Patrick's cabbage, liverworts, mosses and ferns. Tormentil can be found on the moorland slopes, with sundew and butterwort on the boggy patches.

**e** Follow the old track until it rises to the corner of a drystone wall. There are views to the mouth of the fjord, almost blocked by the small island of Inis Bearna. The wall guides the track inland from the sea, making it turn left to descend to a cottage beside a road at Rosroe. Turn right to return to Killary Harbour Youth Hostel.

A dramatically banded sky accompanies the sun setting into the Atlantic Ocean beyond Killary Harbour.

# CLIFDEN & THE FISHERMAN'S TRACK

**START/FINISH:**
The Square, Clifden.

**DISTANCE:** 7½ miles (12km).

**APPROXIMATE TIME:**
4 hours.

**TRANSPORT:**
Mike Nee's Bus and Bus Eireann serve Clifden.

**MAPS:** Harveys Superwalker Connemara; OS Sheets 37 & 44.

**REFRESHMENTS:**
Plenty of shops, pubs and restaurants in and around Clifden.

**ACCOMMODATION:**
Plenty of options from campsites to large hotels in and around Clifden.

Clifden's river is the Owenglin, which rises in the heart of the Twelve Bens, flows out of a boggy glen, past a few farms, skirts the town and debouches through a narrow gorge into Clifden Bay, a spectacular sight when the river is in spate. It's possible to follow the Owenglin River upstream from Clifden, using the nearest roads at first, then faithfully following the banks. Provided that the river is running low, it can be forded and a good track and series of quiet roads can be linked to lead walkers back to Clifden.

## A   The Square, Clifden

Clifden is the activity capital of Connemara with walkers leaving daily for the hills and offshore islands. Sea angling boats head west to rich shark and cod fishing grounds; golfers troop out to a superb links golf course at Ballyconneely. Brown Trout and Salmon anglers make an early start to the numerous lakes and rivers hereabouts.

The village is superbly sited and was well chosen by John D'Arcy when he sought to improve his estate by building here in the early 19th Century. Among its major assets are the superb Natural Harbour of Clifden Bay and the Owenglin River, which provided power for D'Arcy Mills and Brewery and later powered the village's own hydro-electric station, sadly now in ruins. The village follows a classic 19th-Century layout: oval in plan, edging a pre-existing Drumlin Ridge. It has three principal streets, Market Street, Main Street and Bridge Street, a Market Square overlooking the bay, a now-derelict Bridewell and a very fine 19th-Century courthouse. Dominating the town are two imposing 19th Century Churches – Christchurch and St Joseph's. The small Methodist Church is no longer in use and a memorial to Thomas Whelan, a local man executed in 1921 at 20 years old, makes a poignant start to a beautiful cycle route, running west along the now famous Sky Road.

Much of the village was burned to the ground by crowned forces during the War of Independence and was further damaged during the subsequent Civil War. It remained a quiet and poor village until the slow growth of tourism in the 1960s breathed fresh life into Clifden and the surrounding areas. Of the village's most interesting characters was a wise woman

called Cailleach na Libhe who had the power of the curse and the cure. She was a rare survivor of the earlier Celtic traditions of faith healers. People flocked to her to curse their enemies and cure their consumption.

View of the 12 Bens – Binn Bhraoin on the right, Binn Bhán, the highest, in the centre, and Meacanach on the left.

**a** Start in The Square in Clifden and leave the bustling village by way of the Brookside Hostel, Connemara Pony Show Grounds and Station Bar. Follow the course of Low Road, rather than the main Galway road, and turn right as signposted for the Riverview B&B. The road runs close to the Owenglin River and the parallel course of the old railway embankment can be seen; last used in 1937.

## B  The Old Railway
The railway was built in the 1890s by the Congested Districts Board, a Government body tasked with improving social and economic conditions in this populous but poverty-stricken region. Ironically, the section between Ireland and Britain was closed in the 1930s, as population levels fell dramatically due to massive emigration to the industrial cities of England, Scotland and North America, rendering the railway uneconomic.

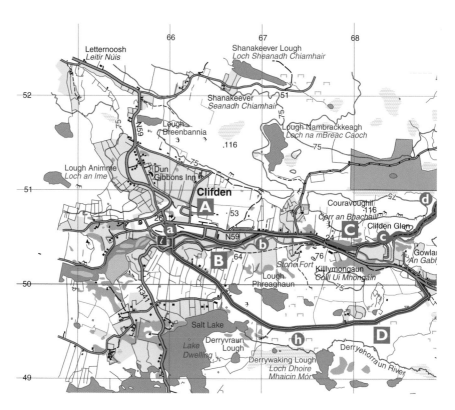

**b** Turn right to follow the main Galway road, though you can also drift left later to follow a loop of old road past Waterloo House and across Waterloo Bridge. Either way, you later reach the access road for the Clifden Glen Holiday Village on the left.

**c** Follow the access road across the Owenglin River, passing the reception, bar and restaurant buildings. Count the chalets on the left up to number 12, then turn left to cross a little footbridge over a stream with a walking man. Follow a path, up a slope of gorse and bracken above the river.

### C Simon's Falls
Below is a series of famous salmon pools known as Simon's Falls. There are big runs from mid-June to July. After heavy rain one can experience the thrill of watching salmon being caught and others jumping the falls, one of the greatest sights one can experience while walking in Connemara.

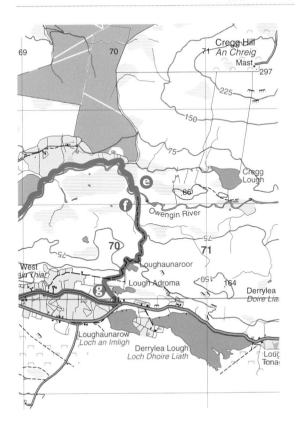

View along the Abhainn Gleann Valley beneath Binn Bhán.

**d** When a series of 'walking man' signs indicate a left turn uphill on a rugged slope, head downhill instead and follow the banks of the Owenglin River upstream. Binn Ghleann Uisce, Binn Bhraoin, and Cregg Hill dominate the view ahead. Stay close to the river to avoid a young forest, and note a couple of farm buildings uphill to the left at Tooraskeheen. A series of pre-bog walls and a 5,000 year-old neolithic tomb have been discovered here in recent years. Later, the river runs deep and straight through a more constricted channel, and where the river describes broader meanders, there is some soft and wet ground to negotiate. In winter, the salmon spawn along this stretch.

**e** Look out for a small sheep pen, because you need to ford the river at this point. There are shoals of gravel and normally the river runs shallow at this point, but please do not cross if the river is running high or if there is any danger of being swept away. You could stop for a while at the nearby Cregg Falls, where salmon lie in pools each summer until floods allow them to proceed further upstream. The mighty Barananoran valley is in front of you, upstream.

**f/g** There is a stony track rising away from the river on the other side, climbing gently up a rugged moorland slope. Again, there are fine views of the Twelve Bens. The track goes through a gate, then loops around the little Loughaunarow. It then descends towards Lough Adroma and swings right, passing a couple of ruined farm buildings and going through a couple more gates. Turn right along a narrow tarmac road and follow it down to the main Clifden to Galway road near Cregg House B&B. Cross over the main road and follow another narrow tarmac road downhill. It later swings right and skirts around the edge of the immense Roundstone Bog, with scores of bog-bound lakes.

### D Roundstone Bog
In June 1919, two British Pilots, John Alcock and Arthur Whitten Brown, ditched their Vickers-Vimmy aircraft here,

West Ridge of Binn Bhán, the highest of the Binns from Binn Fhraoigh.

completing the first ever non-stop Trans-Atlantic Flight. For this they received £10,000 from Lord Beaverbrook and were knighted by the King. A whitewashed tower stands as a reminder of this historic event. The lakes here are a favourite haunt of brown trout fishermen, and, in the winter months, attract migratory white-fronted geese from Greenland. In spring and summer there will be people out cutting and saving turf south of the road. The tarmac gives way to a stony surface near Derrywaking Lough, and extensive views take in the Twelve Bens, Cashel Hill, Errisbeg and Errislannan.

Abandoned hill farm along the river valley.

**h** Pass a Mass Rock, which lies 660ft (200m) south of the road. Mass was said here by the rebel priest Myles Prendergast, who was active during the rebellion of 1798. Follow the track until it climbs high above the Salt Lake, where it becomes a patchy tarmacked road at Dooneen. Dooneen is named after a small and much degraded Iron Age fort to the north. The view westward on the short descent to Clifden is very beautiful. A monument to John D'Arcy over looks the village and the Atlantic stretches off to the horizon. From there, a simple descent leads back into Clifden.

# LEENANE AND LEENANE HILL

**START/FINISH:**
Leenane. The village is at the junction of the main N59 and R336 road near the head of Killary Harbour. There is a car park beside Killary Harbour opposite the Leenane Cultural Centre.

**DISTANCE:** 7 miles (11km).

**APPROXIMATE TIME:** 4 hours.

**HIGHEST POINT:** 2030ft (618m) on the summit of Leenane Hill.

**MAPS:** Harveys Superwalker Connemara; OS Sheet 37.

**REFRESHMENTS:** There are a few pubs and restaurants offering food and drink in Leenane, as well as the Leenane Cultural Centre.

**ADVICE:** Leenane Hill is broad-shouldered, steep-sided and mostly grassy. It might seem featureless in mist, but on this route most of the circuit is accomplished following high-level fences, which are sure guides in poor visibility.

Rising south of Leenane village, Leenane Hill spreads sprawling shoulders in all directions. Although it lies at the northern end of the Maum Turk Mountains, it shares nothing with the rest of this rugged range. The underlying rocks are sedimentary, part of a series laid down in the Silurian period, breaking down to allow good grass cover instead of bare rock and scree. As a viewpoint, Leenane Hill is superb, taking in mountains in both Connemara and neighbouring Mayo. The route begins and ends with clear tracks, while fences offer sure guides in between. This is prime sheep country and the growth of the woollen industry can be appreciated by visiting the Sheep and Wool Museum at the Leenane Cultural Centre.

The rugged, lumpy flanks of Leenane Hill rise above Leenane village and the waters of Killary Harbour.

**A    A Lamb's Tale (from the Sheep and Wool Museum)**

A travelling priest once came to Connemara and was surprised to meet a sheep farmer who did not even know one prayer. 'I will teach you a prayer,' said the priest, 'and when I return next year I expect you to remember it.'

The prayer he taught the farmer was: 'A Uain Dé a thógas peacaí an domhain déan trocaire orainn.' (Lamb of God who takes away the sins of the world have mercy on us.)

As promised the priest returned one year later and he asked the farmer to repeat the prayer. The farmer said, 'A Uascáin Dé a thógas peacaí an domhain déan trocaire orainn.' (Hogget of God who takes away the sins of the world have mercy on us.)

'No, no,' said the priest. 'It is not "a Uascáin Dé", it is "a Uain Dé".'

'But Father,' said the farmer, 'if he was "a uain" (lamb) last year he would have to be "a uascáin" (hogget) this year!'

a    Leave the village of Leenane by following the main N59 road in the direction of Letterfrack. This road passes a couple of restaurants, B&Bs and the Leenane Inn. Pass the last building in the village and continue along the road beside Killary Harbour. On the left is a track serving a tall communications mast, and there is a signpost indicating the course of the Western Way.

A grassy, boggy moorland crest is followed around a huge semi-circular coum to reach the top of Leenane Hill.

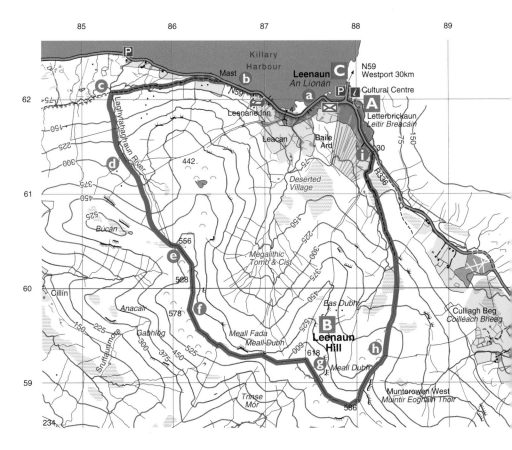

**b** Climb a stile beside a gate near the communications mast and continue along a grassy and stony track. The track runs across a large, square enclosure surrounded by a drystone wall, so one more stile has to be crossed, beside another gate. The steep slopes rising from Killary Harbour are scattered with boulders and vegetated with grass and bracken. Looking ahead Mweelrea rises from Killary Harbour, with Binn Gorm seen directly across the water, and the Devilsmother rises back towards the head of the inlet. Cross a stile beside a gate in a fence, then cross a stream using a culvert bridge.

**c** Turn left to start walking upstream. The fence runs parallel to the stream and there are a whole series of little waterfalls to admire. The slope bears a few small boulders, grass and bracken, but progress uphill is easy. Later, the way is mostly grassy, a little boggy underfoot, and the fence switches to the far side of the stream. There is no need to cross the stream, and there are scanty traces of a path to follow in any case. Looking back along the valley, there are good views through the deeply-cut Doo Lough Pass between Binn Gorm and Mweelrea, north of Killary Harbour.

**d** The gradient eases a little in a higher part of the valley, and a rash of large boulders turn out to be coarse, boulder conglomerates. Keep following the stream and fence more steeply up the grassy slope at the head of the valley to emerge on a boggy gap near Búcán with a sudden, superb view of the Twelve Bens, after the restricted views in the valley. The hills are well displayed, including Binn Dhoire Chláir, Binn Chorr, Binn Bhraoin, Binn Dhubh, Binn Bhán, Binn Fhraoigh, Meacanach, An Chailleach, Binn Bhreac, Maolan and Diamond Hill. Also seen across Kylemore Lough are Dúchruach, Binn Fhraoigh and Maolchnoc.

**e** Cross the fence on the gap and climb to the little summit to the left, which is marked by a small cairn at 183ft (556m). Below in the valley in the remains of a deserted hamlet, lies a ruined cist and a chambered tomb. There is a fine view back over to Leenane, including the head of Killary Harbour and the Devilsmother. To continue, drop down to the next boggy gap and follow the fence onwards.

**f** The next rise bears a few low outcrops of rock, but is also quite boggy in places. The fence describes a broad arc around a huge mountain hollow on the way to Leenane Hill. Looking around this hollow, a feature of note is An Briseadh Mór, or the Big Break, where a huge chunk of rock collapsed, leaving a hole in the hillside and a prominent bouldery tongue of scree. Ravens may be observed testing the thermals all the way around the edge. The line of the fence leads unerringly, via a leftward spur, to the top of Leenane Hill.

**B   Leenane Hill 874593**
The summit of Leenane Hill bears a cairn at 2032ft (618m). Views are remarkably extensive, among the best in Connemara, taking in the Devilsmother, Mám Trasna and Maolan at the end of Loch na Fuaiche. Bunnacunneen and a portion of Lough Corrib are seen, then Leac Aimhréidh, Binn Mhór and the gap of Máméan. Binn Idir an Dá Log and Binn Bhriocáin are followed by the gap of Mám Tuirc. The Twelve Bens have already been noted, though Binn Gabhar is now also distinguished. Dúchruach, Binn Fhraoigh and Maolchnoc are followed by a view beyond Killary Harbour to the island of Inis Tuirc.

Looking back to the broad summit of Leenane Hill before commencing a steep and grassy descent.

Mweelrea is followed by the gap of the Doo Lough Pass, with a view through to Achill Island. Nearby Binn Gorm and the Sheeffry Hills are followed by more distant Croagh Patrick and Nephin, as well as some small hills north of Castlebar, such as Croaghmoyle and Burren Mountain.

**g** Step over the fence beside the cairn and walk roughly south-east from the summit of Leenane Hill, not necessarily following the circuitous course taken by the line of the fence across this broad, bleak crest. There are grassy as well as gravelly areas, and some parts are boggy. The fence leads along the broad crest, then swings to the left to start a steep descent. Walk down the grassy slope alongside the fence, aiming almost northwards at the start. Further downhill, there are low rocky outcrops. The fence veers off to the right and is no longer a useful guide.

**h** There is an almost level shoulder on the hummocky ridge, followed by another steep descent, very slippery in wet weather, with some rocky outcrops. Look for a line of old fenceposts off, a little to the left, and follow them for a while. Later, these veer to the right, so drift left again to locate an old grassy track leading down from a series of old turf cuttings. The track runs down alongside a river, where a large waterfall might be noticed. There are smaller waterfalls at a lower level, as well as old field systems across the valley. A line of mixed trees are noticed before the track runs down to the R336 road.

**i** Turn left to follow the road across a bridge and down into Leenane. Note the flowery gardens of Casa de Flores, as well as a couple of B&Bs and the Michael Davitt Memorial Hall in a former National School building.

### C  Leenane 878619

Formerly, Leenane's full name was Líonán Cinn Mhara, or the Shoal at the Head of the Sea. The Joyce's and the King's were notable families who contributed to the development of the area. While touring Connemara in 1903, King Edward VII and Queen Alexandra stayed at the Leenane Inn, the largest hotel in the area. A quick tour of the village is easily accomplished, taking in its pubs, restaurants, shops and accommodation options. Leenane is one of the principal gateways to Connemara. There are ample reminders, particularly at Hamilton's Bar, of the filming of John B. Keane's intensely passionate story of *The Field* which starred Richard Harris.

Looking back up towards Leenane Hill from a point on the grassy track near the village.

# LEENANE & CNOC AN DOIRÍN

**START/FINISH:**
Leenane. The village is at the junction of the main N59 and R336 roads near the head of Killary Harbour. There is a car park beside Killary Harbour opposite the Leenane Cultural Centre.

**DISTANCE:** 10 miles (16km).

**APPROXIMATE TIME:** 5 hours.

**HIGHEST POINT:**
1970ft (600m) on a broad, nameless summit on the south-eastern shoulder of Leenane Hill.

**MAPS:** Harveys Superwalker Connemara; OS Sheet 37.

**REFRESHMENTS:**
The Maam Country Knitwear shop offers refreshments just off route when the route descends from Cnoc an Doirín, otherwise there are plenty of places offering food and drink back at Leenane.

**ADVICE:**
This hill walk is fairly straight forward, with fences offering good guides along a boggy crest. Note that the ascent is steep and the descent is very steep, with a small, hidden, greasy cliff needing care. A river crossing following the descent could be impassable after heavy rain, in which case a nearby farm road bridge would need to be used.

The territory of Connemara ends alongside Joyce's River. The river flows through a valley on a major fault line which can be traced northwards through the Doo Lough Pass and southwards to Lough Corrib. There is a range of grassy hills on the southern side of the valley, which can be climbed from the village of Leenane. Strangely, the hills are practically nameless, although the most northerly one is generally called Leenane Hill, while the most southerly is Cnoc an Doirín. A walk along this grassy, boggy crest is easy enough in clear weather, though there is a steep ascent and descent. In mist, almost the whole route can be completed by using the lines of prominent fences as guides.

**A   Leenane Cultural Centre 878619**
In the 19th Century, sheep were described as 'longwools' and 'shortwools'. In Connemara the little primitive shortwools were known as Claddagh sheep. The large longwool Roscommon was bred by crossing native sheep with Border Leicester and Oxford Down, with further refinements creating the large, stocky Galway breed. In the years after the Great Famine, around 1850–70, landlords transported Scottish Blackface into the area and they have dominated the western mountains ever since. Breeders have resisted the introduction of Blackface sheep bred in lowland areas, thereby maintaining a stock of hardy sheep well-used to mountain conditions. The Leenane Cultural Centre incorporates a Sheep and Wool Museum, with information on breeds, a sample of spinning wheels and looms, examples of knitting and specific information on the area around Leenane. There are different breeds of sheep grazing outside the centre. Nearby is a green building still known as Joyce's Wool Store.

**a**   Follow the road signposted for Mám, passing a number of houses and a handful of B&Bs, as well as the Michael Davitt Memorial Hall in a former National School. Cross the bridge at the upper end of the village, then immediately turn right along a clear, grassy track. Follow the track upstream, passing trees and a concrete water tank. There are a series of small waterfalls along the stream. This is dipper habitat: it prefers fast-flowing water as it dives for aquatic invertebrates. There are views back towards Binn Gorm from the higher parts of the track, which expires in an area of old turf cuttings.

A couple of walkers climb the grassy slopes of Leenane Hill above the village of Leenane.

**b**   A line of old fenceposts beside a boggy groove can be followed further uphill, ending at a steeply inclined rock slab. Above the slab is a boggy shoulder, then a series of low, inclined rock slab outcrops. A fence runs steeply up a grassy slope, reaching a junction with another fence near the top of the slope. In clear weather, it is worth turning right to reach the summit of Leenane Hill, where a superb all-round view can be enjoyed, which will not be equalled on any part of the route detailed below. To continue with this route, however, turn left at the fence junction. Look out for snipes and ravens.

**c**   The fence leads gradually downhill along a broad crest of decaying blanket bog. There are some exposed stony areas, but no clear path. In good visibility, make the most of the

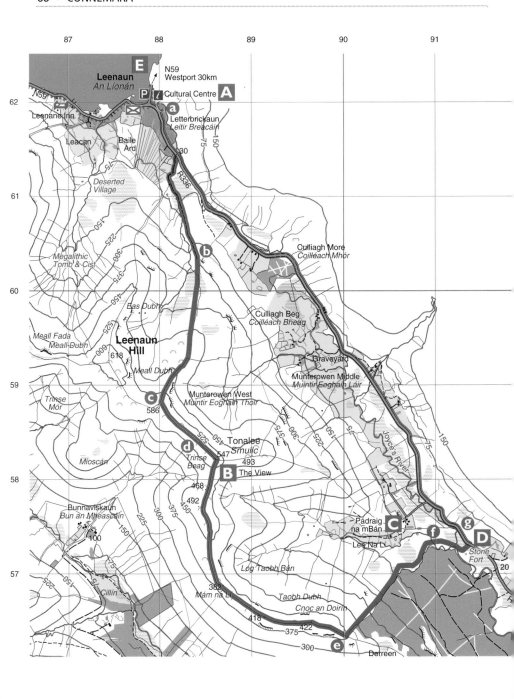

views and walk along the broad crest, otherwise stay close to the fence. After crossing a boggy gap, the next grassy dome bears a small pool and another junction of fences.

### B   The View 886583

There are views of Leic Aimhréidh and the Maum Turk Mountains through to Binn Bhriocáin and Binn Mhór. The Twelve Bens feature everything from Binn Chorr to Diamond Hill, with Dúchruach and Maolchnoc beyond Kylemore. Binn Log Mhór, Binn Gorm, Sheeffry Hills, Croagh Patrick and the Devilsmother are all in view, along with Bunnacunneen, Lugnabrick and Lough Corrib.

The line of a fence provides a useful guide along the broad crest from Leenane Hill to Cnoc an Doirín.

**d**   Turn right and follow the fence downhill, crossing a ruined fence on a boggy gap. Climb uphill and follow all the twists and turns made by the fence as it climbs up the next slope. There are fine views over into Gleann Glaise, with its large, remote farmstead. Much of the glen has been drained and recently planted with forest. The last wolf in Connemara is supposed to have been slain in Gleann Glaise. This valley is extremely rich in Bronze Age settlement and ritual monuments. Keep your eyes peeled for white quartz stone row appearing out of the bog and a stone pair at the valley entrance and continue downhill on another grassy slope, crossing a fence before reaching the next gap. Follow the fence uphill, further along the crest, crossing one last broad rise at Cnoc an Doirín. It is a good idea to cross the fence and then look over the edge of the hill down towards Joyce's River.

A herd of goats may be encountered at the foot of Cnoc an Doirín on the way to Joyce's River.

**e** There is a spur from the fence on Cnoc an Doirín, heading downhill to the left, running alongside a forest. The slope is steep and grassy, needing great care where a wet and slippery cliff-line appears almost without warning. Stay close to the forest fence, or keep well away to the left to pass this obstacle. The damp, dripping cliff affords a foothold away from grazing sheep to a number of plants, such as St. Patrick's cabbage, spleenwort, butterwort, mosses and ferns. Continue downhill and cross another fence, keeping close to the edge of the forest. There is tussocky grassy bog and bog myrtle, with some very soft, muddy patches in places. There may be a herd of goats in the area.

### C   Pádraig na mBán
During the dark years of the Great Famine, 1845–8, a well-to-do farmer lived in this valley. He took in a dozen dispossessed young women and kept each one in a small cabin. He is said to have fathered a child by each one of them and is remembered as Pádraig na mBán, or Patrick of the Women.

**f** Follow a small stream alongside the forest, passing around the lower, clear-felled parts. Walk downstream alongside Joyce's River after crossing a fence spanning the river. If possible, cross the river at a handy shoal of gravel, otherwise continue downstream to cross at a ford on the forest access track. Either way, the idea is to reach a ringfort on top of a low, grassy hillock. Note that after heavy rain Joyce's River might prove impassable, both at the gravel shoal and at the ford used by the forest track. The only useful bridge is upstream on a farm access track.

### D   The Ringfort 914573
The ringfort sits as a stony heap on top of a grassy hillock beside Joyce's River. The cobbly circular rampart seems to have been reworked into a drystone wall in recent years, though the basic structure is centuries old. The ringfort will have been a defensive farmstead, probably occupied by an extended family, featuring a wooden palisade and internal hut structures. Ringforts were common in Ireland during the early Christian period.

**g** Walk to the R336 road. There used to be a stile over the roadside fence. Either turn right to reach the Maam Country Knitwear shop, which offers refreshments, or turn left to follow the road back to Leenane. If a lift can be arranged back to Leenane, then the walk can end at this point. There is only one bus service a week through the valley. The road is gently graded and passes only a handful of houses and farms. Practically the whole of the road is enclosed by fences and there is one small forest plantation which is passed. The road squeezes through a gap, passing a cute little cottage where photography is expressly forbidden, according to a roadside sign! The road runs down to the bridge which was crossed earlier in the day, and continues back down into Leenane. The village has a few places offering food and drink.

### E   Leenane 878619

Formerly, Leenane's full name was Líonán Cinn Mhara, or the Shoal at the Head of the Sea. The Joyce's and the King's were notable families who contributed to the development of the area. While touring Connemara in 1903, King Edward VII and Queen Alexandra stayed at the Leenane Inn, the largest hotel in the area. A quick tour of the village is easily accomplished, taking in its pubs, restaurants, shops and accommodation options. Leenane is one of the principal gateways to Connemara. There are ample reminders, particularly at Hamilton's Bar, of the filming of John B. Keane's intensely passionate story of *The Field* which starred Richard Harris.

Part of the stone wall which encircles the ringfort between Joyce's River and the road.

# GLEANN CREAMHA & MÁM TUIRC

**START/FINISH:**
At the junction of the main N59 road and the access road for Gleann Creamha. There is a small parking space beside the junction.

**DISTANCE:** 12½ miles (20km).

**APPROXIMATE TIME:**
7 hours.

**HIGHEST POINT:**
1906ft (578m) on a broad, nameless summit near Leenane Hill.

**MAPS:** Harveys Superwalker Connemara; OS Sheet 37.

**REFRESHMENTS:**
None on the route. Leenane can be reached via the main road alongside Killary Harbour and the Pass Inn Hotel is at Kylemore in the opposite direction.

**ADVICE:**
Virtually the whole upland circuit has fences as guides. The lower parts have clear, waymarked paths and tracks. Some parts can be quite wet and boggy.

**G**leann Creamha is at the northern end of the Maum Turk Mountain range, surrounded on all sides by steep-sided grassy slopes and occupied by two isolated farms. A walk around Gleann Creamha can be structured to start and finish on the waymarked Western Way. The ascent takes in steep-sided Búcán and runs almost to Leenane Hill, but then there is a drop to a low-slung gap with another ascent beyond. Binn Bhán is rockier, but relatively easy, with a descent to the gap of Mám Tuirc. A series of old paths and tracks can be combined on the descent to make the route into a circuit.

**a** Start on the main N59 road between Leenane and Kylemore, where a minor road is marked only with a signpost for the Glen Valley Farmhouse B&B. This turning is near a bridge and a small stand of pine trees. There is a small space to park cars near some bouldery rubble at the junction. Walk up the narrow road to a forest, then turn left along a stony track just outside the forest.

**b** At the corner of the forest, start climbing up the slopes of Búcán alongside the forest fence. The line of the fence continues high above the forest, and as parts of the fence have

rusted, beware of the loops and strands which litter the hillside. The slope is steep and grassy, with a few rocks poking through, and some parts are quite wet. There is a hummocky shoulder, where a pause for breath reveals that views are opening up very well. As the fence climbs higher, it swings to the right and is no longer a useful guide. Climb straight uphill, crossing some rather wet areas, until a tiny cairn is reached on top of Búcán.

## A   Búcán 853697

After all the effort of the steep ascent, there is a rewarding view from the top of Búcán, whose altitude is 1822ft (550m). The view takes in the sprawling shoulders of Leenane Hill, tracking around the Maum Turk Mountains to embrace Binn Idir an Dá Log, Binn Mhór and Binn Bhriocáin. The Twelve Bens feature Binn Dhoire Chláir, Binn Chorr, Binn Bhraoin, Binn Dhubh, Binn Bhán, Binn Fhraoigh, Meacanach, An Chailleach, Binn Bhreac, Maolan and Diamond Hill. Seen across Kylemore Lough are Dúchruach, Maolchnoc and Binn Mhór. Across Killary Harbour are Mweelrea, Sheeffry Hills and Binn Gorm.

From a point along the broad and boggy crest there is a view back through the Doo Lough Pass.

Looking back towards the steep flanks of Búcán with Maolchnoc and Kylemore seen in the distance.

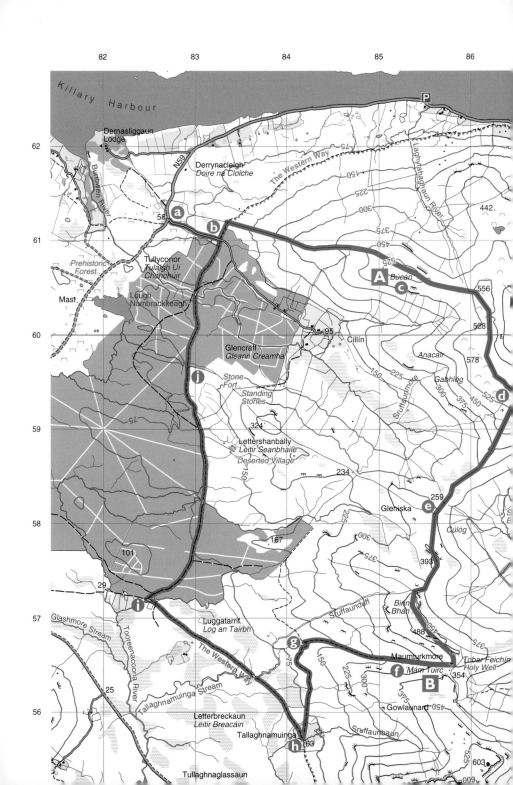

**c** Walk across the top of Búcán and cross a broad and boggy gap to reach the corner of a fence on the far side. Keep always to the right side of the fence, unless a view over to Leenane is required. The fence heads off to the right and crosses a boggy gap. The next broad rise on the crest bears a few low outcrops of rock, but remains boggy in places. Follow the fence faithfully until there is a junction with another fence, then turn right to start descending towards a low-slung gap. (An extension could take the route onto Leenane Hill for a wide-ranging view in clear weather.)

**d** The fence runs down a steep and grassy slope, though there are a few very steep sections where rock is also exposed. The fence is a sure guide in mist, and its middle reaches are accompanied by the ruins of a drystone wall. Be wary of loops of rusting wire strewn across the slope. The fence runs out onto a hummocky, boggy gap, with Gleann Creamha to the right and Gleann Glaise to the left and the prehistoric enclosure.

**e** Follow the fence straight up a steep, grassy slope above the gap. There is a little dip on the way uphill, and another fence needs to be stepped across. The fence then swings left as it cuts across one side of the crest. There is another little dip, then the fence climbs a steep slope of grass and moss, avoiding a steeper, rockier slope. At the top, cross a stile at a junction of fences and turn left. In mist, the fence is a sure guide to the next gap, Mám Tuirc, but it misses the jagged, rocky summit of Binn Bhán, which is worth a visit in clear weather. The Ordnance Survey calls this summit Maumturkmore.

### B Mám Tuirc 857565

The whole of the Maum Turk Mountains have been named after this gap, which means the Pass of the Boar. Just on the eastern side of the gap, near the fence, is a small holy well dedicated to St. Feichin. It is situated beside a cairn, and without this marker it might easily be missed altogether. The historian Roderick O'Flaherty mentioned it very briefly: 'There is a well in memorie of St. Fechin at Mam-tuirk.'

**f** Descend westwards from the gap of Mám Tuirc, following a rugged valley downhill with views towards Kylemore Lough. Look carefully for traces of an old path which crosses the pass, which is still distinguishable with care. It runs close to a stream, (where butterworts grow) then drifts a little away from it later. Watch carefully as there is an intersection with another old track, which is followed by turning left, crossing the stream.

The waymarked Western Way leads across a broad area of bog, offering views towards the Kylemore Pass.

**g** Follow the lower track carefully around a spur, passing a small ruin, noting that the surface becomes wider and the track becomes more obvious. It appears to have been a Famine Relief Road, as it runs nowhere in particular. It shows many signs of engineering, but also has some rugged uncut sections and heaps of boulders, suggesting that it was never finished. The track runs across a bog at the foot of the mountains, then reaches a fence. Turn right to follow the fence to a gate and stile on an adjacent track. Spotters here will notice skylarks, wheatears and snipes.

**h** Turn right to follow this broader track, which is the course of the Western Way. It is firm and grassy at first, but becomes boggier later, reaching another gate and stile. Cross a footbridge over a river to continue. The track is broad and firm again, but becomes quite wet and muddy before reaching a stand of forest. Cross a river beside the forest, then turn right to enter the forest crossing a stile beside a gate, where crossbills and siskins are at home.

**i** Follow the forest track gently uphill, avoiding both a left and a right turn, to reach the end of the track. Cross a stile where there is a Western Way marker post and cross a bridge over the river draining Gleann Uisce. A broad, clear path continues across the rugged slope just above the forest. Cross a rise, noting a series of old enclosures and ruins to the right at Lettershanbally. Incidentally, Leitir Seanbhaile means the Hillside of the Old Settlement. A short detour northwest leads to a beautiful ridge and rough track used for pony trekking. The panoramic views take in the O'Neill Farm and a standing stone and cashel (fort).

After crossing another stile, look out for a coarse bouldery conglomerate rock. The next stile takes the Western Way back into the forest.

j   Follow a broad forest ride, which is covered in long grass, rushes and bog myrtle. There is a trodden path, but this is wet and muddy in places. The forest ride undulates, then drops down to a river, which is crossed by a footbridge. Note the invasive giant rhubarb growing along the riverbanks. After crossing the bridge, follow a forest track gently uphill. There is more giant rhubarb beside the track before a gate and stile are reached. Turn left along a narrow tarmac road to leave the forest, following the road gently downhill to return to the main road where the walk started.

The waymarked Western Way leads through forest at Lettershanbally to return to Gleann Creamha.

# BINN BHRIOCÁIN AND MÁM TUIRC

**START/FINISH:**
On a minor road, on the Western Way, above the Lough Inagh Lodge in the Inagh Valley. This prominent hotel stands on the R344 road between Kylemore and Recess.

**DISTANCE:** 10 miles (16km).

**APPROXIMATE TIME:** 6 hours.

**HIGHEST POINT:** 2193ft (667m) on the summit of Binn Bhriocáin.

**MAPS:** Harveys Superwalker Connemara; OS Sheet 37.

**REFRESHMENTS:**
None on the route, though the Lough Inagh Lodge is close to the start. There is also the Inagh Valley Inn in one direction along the R344 road and the Pass Inn Hotel at the junction of the R344 and the main N59 road.

**ADVICE:**
The summits and gaps along the Maum Turk Mountain range are awkwardly arranged. In mist it will be necessary to take frequent compass bearings. Some of the rivers crossed by the Western Way can become quite swollen after heavy rain and may prove impossible to cross dry-shod.

The middle reaches of the Maum Turk Mountain range are readily accessible from the Inagh Valley and the Western Way. There are two main summits and two significant gaps which can be linked with low-level roads and bog roads to form a fine circuit. In clear weather the ridge offers exhilarating walking, but it is all rough and rocky. In poor visibility map and compass skills will be required as there are several changes of direction. There is a small holy well dedicated to St. Feichin on the gap of Mám Tuirc; the gap from which the entire mountain range takes its name. The other gap of Mám Ochóige is on an excavated fault line.

Cnoc na hUilleann appears as a huge rocky dome when seen from the lower slopes near the road.

## A   Bun na gCroc

Bun na gCroc, which translates as the Foot of the Hill, is the name of the Gaeltacht, or Irish speaking area, which encompasses all the little farmsteads between the Maum Turk Mountains and Cnoc Lios Uachtair.

a   When driving through the Inagh Valley, there is a minor road signposted for Máméan near the Lough Inagh Lodge. Follow this road uphill to park in a small roadside space near a signpost indicating the course of the Western Way. Continuing on foot, follow the minor road over a rise, passing a few little farmsteads, then descend through a boggy area to cross a bridge over a river. The river flows down from the gap of Mám Ochóige, which is the key to the ascent on this particular walk.

b   Once across the bridge, turn left to leave the road and start walking across a broad, boggy slope. While it is possible to follow the river upstream, it may be better to walk somewhat to the right of the river, climbing gradually up a boggy, grassy slope where sundew and marsh violets grow. There are a few inflowing streams to cross, and there are boulders scattered all around the mountainous hollow; dippers enjoy the little waterfalls. On the ascent, look across the stream to spot an area of old 'lazy beds' where potatoes were once grown. Climb steeply up a grassy slope peppered with boulders to emerge on a grassy gap crossed by a fence. Looking back, Cnoc Lios Uachtair is finely framed by the valley, with Loch Leitheanach at its foot. Irish hares live in this habitat, as do ravens.

A fence runs across the top of the gap of Mám Ochóige. A left turn here leads up onto Cnoc na hUilleann.

## B   Mám Ochóige 877537

Mám Ochóige is Anglicised as Maumohoge: there is no clear translation of the name. The gap itself is fairly nondescript. The lovely Loch Mhám Ochóige is not actually on the gap, but

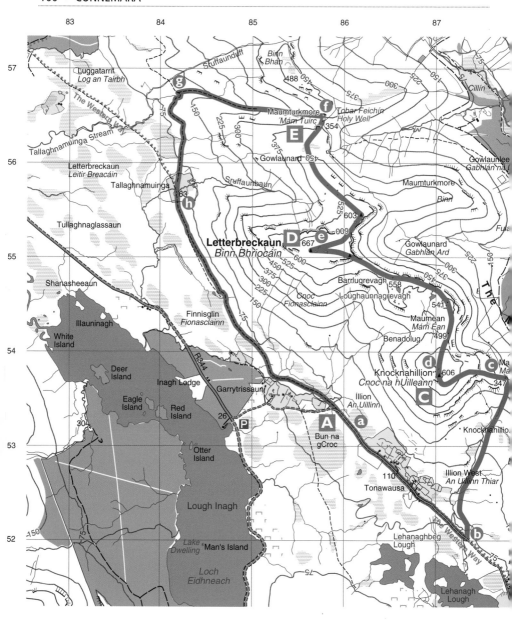

is couched in a rocky bowl a short way uphill to the east. It will be seen by looking back across the gap during the ascent of Cnoc na hUilleann.

Seen from the Western Way at the foot of the mountain, Binn Bhriocáin appears very steep and rugged.

c   Turn left at the gap of Mám Ochóige and climb steeply up a slope of grass, heather and low outcrops of quartzite. The whole slope is scattered with broken rock. Looking back, Loch Mhám Ochoige can be seen. Continue climbing uphill from a shoulder, and a short stretch of gravelly path leads over the summit of Cnoc na hUilleann.

## C   Cnoc na hUilleann 870537

Cnoc na hUilleann, Anglicised as Knocknahillion, is the Hill of the Elbow. Its situation on the Mám Tuirc ridge is rather like a projecting elbow, and there is a significant change of direction on the summit. The view takes in a fine sweep of the Twelve Bens across the Inagh Valley, followed by Dúchruach and Maolchnoc, Binn Bhriocáin, Mweelrea, Leenane Hill, Devilsmother, Mám Trasna, Bunnacunneen, Benlevy, Cnoc na gCorr, Binn Idir an Dá Log, Cashel Hill and Errisbeg.

**d** A cairn close to the summit cairn shows the direction towards the next gap. Walk down a slope of broken rock and low outcrops. There is another cairn just before the gap. A trodden path slices across the flanks of the next rocky rise, keeping to the left, though some walkers may prefer to cross over it. The broad summit bears a cairn. The gap beyond is marked by a pool, which can be passed on the right. Climb uphill on a rocky ridge to reach the broad, stony summit area of Binn Bhriocáin. Pass to the left of two pools to reach the summit cairn.

### D Binn Bhriocáin 855551
Anglicised as Letterbreckaun, Binn Bhriocáin appears to be named after a person called Briocán, but nothing more is known of his identity. The summit rises to 2193ft (667m). There is a considerable rocky slope dropping steeply to an almost level stretch of bog in the Inagh Valley. Do not be tempted to make a direct descent, even in an emergency.

**e** Leaving the summit, keep to the left of another pool and cross a rugged hump. The slope downhill is rough, rocky and stony, leading to a small pool on a gap. A short climb leads up to a little summit with a cairn. Swing left to follow a rocky ridge, but later drift to the right towards the low gap of Mám Tuirc. Take special care on the descent towards the gap, as there are hidden cliffs and slippery slopes. Aim towards the fence which crosses the eastern side of the gap and a vague path will be found outflanking any difficulties.

### E Mám Tuirc 857565
The whole of the Maum Turk Mountains have been named after this gap, which means the Pass of the Boar. Just on the eastern side of the gap, near the fence, is a small holy well dedicated to St. Feichin. It is situated beside a cairn, and without this marker it might easily be missed altogether. The historian Roderick O'Flaherty mentioned it very briefly: 'There is a well in memorie of St. Fechin at Mam-tuirk.'

**f** Descend westwards from the gap of Mám Tuirc, following a rugged valley downhill with fine views towards Kylemore Lough. Look carefully for traces of an old path which crosses the pass: this is still distinguishable with care, running close to a stream, (where butterworts grow) then drifting a little away from it later to cross inflowing streams with greater ease. Watch carefully as there is an intersection with another old track, which is followed by turning left, crossing the stream.

**g** Follow the lower track carefully around a spur, passing a small ruin, noting that the surface becomes wider and the track more obvious. It appears to have been a Famine Relief Road, as it runs nowhere in particular. Although it shows many signs of engineering, it has some rugged uncut sections and heaps of boulders, suggesting that it was never finished. The track runs across a bog at the foot of the mountains, then reaches a fence. Turn right to follow the fence to a gate and stile on an adjacent track. The birdlife thriving in the area includes skylark, wheatear and snipe.

**h** Cross the stile beside the gate to follow an even broader and much clearer track. This is the course of the Western Way, passing a ruined limekiln, just to the left, and heading towards another gate and stile. The track crosses a bleak and boggy area at the foot of the mountains, crossing streams by fords or

The waymarked Western Way leads through the boggy Inagh Valley to bring the walk to a close.

culverts. Be careful not to be drawn along a parallel track to the right, which ends in very soft bog. The track runs close to some houses, then crosses a couple of larger rivers, which may carry a a considerable flow of water after heavy rain, before climbing up to a minor road. The minor road is the point at which the walk started, so reaching it brings the circuit to a close.

# MÁMÉAN AND BINN IDIR AN DÁ LOG

**START/FINISH:**
At a car park at the foot of Máméan. Roads running to Máméan are well signposted from the main N59 road near Recess and from the R344 road in the Inagh Valley.

**DISTANCE:** 8 miles (13km).

**APPROXIMATE TIME:**
4 hours.

**HIGHEST POINT:**
2307ft (702m) on the summit of Binn Idir an Dá Log, which is the highest of the Maum Turk Mountains.

**MAPS:** Harveys Superwalker Connemara; OS Sheets 37 & 44.

**REFRESHMENTS:**
None on the route. The minor road can be followed one way to the R344 road and the Lough Inagh Lodge, or the other way to the main N59 road and to Paddy Festy's at Recess, where food and drink can be obtained.

**ADVICE:**
The lower parts of this walk are without real difficulty, but careful navigation is needed over the mountains, especially in mist. The descent to Mám Ochóige is particularly steep and rocky, and can become quite slippery when wet.

Binn Idir an Dá Log is the highest of the Maum Turk Mountains and is situated roughly in the centre of the range. An ascent and descent can be based on the two nearest prominent gaps in the range; Máméan and Mám Ochóige. Both gaps have been formed on excavated fault lines in the quartzite bedrock. The gap of Máméan is a regular crossroads for walkers as it is crossed by the waymarked Western Way and the annual Maum Turks Walk. The traverse of Binn Idir an Dá Log is as rough as any walk in the Maum Turk Mountains, and the descent to Mám Ochóige is quite steep and rocky, with only a limited choice of routes.

The Patrician pilgrimage path is flanked by kerbstones so that its course is clearly defined over Máméan.

**a**   Máméan is signposted from Recess on the main N59 road, as well as from the R344 road near the Lough Inagh Lodge. There is a car park at the foot of the track leading to the gap, and another signpost pointing into the hills, indicating both the direction of Máméan and the Western Way. Follow the grassy track uphill, crossing a stile beside an iron gate. The gate is also marked with the name Máméan. The track crosses a small stream and runs further uphill. It is sometimes grassy and sometimes stony, but nearly always flanked by kerbstones, with occasional Western Way marker posts bearing yellow arrows. The track runs on bare rock towards the top, then the Chapel, Statue and Stations of the Cross come into view to the left.

### A   Máméan 905504

Máméan is Anglicised as Maumeen and means the Pass of the Birds. Roderick O'Flaherty wrote of the place: 'At Mamen, there springs out of a stone a litle water, named from St. Patrick, which is a present remedy against murrein in cattel, not only applyed, but alsoe as soon as tis sent for they begin to have ease.' The pilgrimage site features a small chapel called Cillín Phádraig; a covered altar called Carraig Aifrinn Phádraig Naofa; Leaba Phádraig, or St. Patrick's Bed; Tobar Phádraig, or St. Patrick's Well; Buntobar Phádraig Naofa, another holy well; a statue inscribed Pádraig Mór na hÉireann; and the Stations of the Cross in a wide anti-clockwise circuit around the site. Note the Connemara Marble on the altar and the lovely collection of ferns growing behind it. It is said that St. Patrick reached the summit of the pass, but did not cross over it. Instead, he blessed the outlying regions of Connemara from it. The pilgrimage had been abandoned, but has been revived in recent years, as the dedication dates on the various structures attest, running from 1980–93.

Binn Mhairg is a subsidiary summit close to Binn Chaonaigh. Its slopes are very steep and rocky.

**b**   There is a fence crossing the gap at Máméan. Turn left to follow it uphill, climbing steeply on a bouldery slope and steep grass. There is an easier shoulder, then more climbing up rugged ground. Looking at dark and damp crevices in the

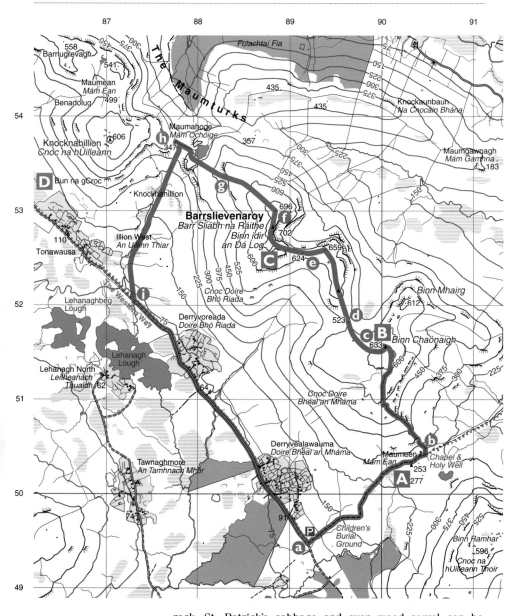

rock, St. Patrick's cabbage and even wood sorrel can be spotted. The fence twists and turns, but is a good guide in mist. The gradient eases on a hummocky slope of decaying blanket bog. The fence heads off to the right without reaching the summit of Binn Chaonaigh, so leave it to make a summit bid. There is a cairn beyond a pool of water.

**B Binn Chaonaigh 900515**
Binn Chaonaigh means Mossy Peak. In mist it needs a little care as there are two cairned summits as well as the rounded, rocky summit of Binn Mhairg overlooking Gleann Fhada. The whole summit area is a jumble of low rocky outcrops, heaps of stones and patches of heather and crowberry. The highest cairn stands at 2076ft (633m).

**c** Take care over the descent. There is an indistinct path on crunchy quartzite gravel running down to the next gap. The path crosses some bare rock and patches of heather, and the terrain remains the same all the way across the gap.

**d** The ascent from the gap is on grass, heather and boulders, becoming rather more rocky with height. The next part of the ridge is hummocky rock. Some walkers stay high on the ridge, while others side-step it to the left. There is a small cairn on one rocky hump on the ridge then a short, steep descent leads down to a little gap.

**e** Walkers generally keep to the left of the next broken rock ridge, following a clear band of white quartz uphill. There is a cairned summit just to the right towards the top. The rest of the rugged crest is broad and hummocky, covered in broken rock, stones and heather. There is a final, short, rocky climb passing a streak of quartz to reach the summit cairn on Binn Idir an Dá Log.

**C Binn Idir an Dá Log 888528**
The highest point in the Maum Turk Mountains remains nameless on Ordnance Survey maps, but it is known as Binn Idir an Dá Log, or the Peak Between Two Hollows. The summit cairn stands at 2307ft (702m). Views embrace the solitary Cnoc Lios Uachtair and Cashel Hill, the latter seen across Roundstone Bog. After Ballynahinch Lough come the Twelve Bens, which feature Binn Dhoire Chláir, Binn Gabhar, Binn Braoin, Binn Chorr, Binn Dhubh, Binn Bhán, Binn Bhreac and Maolan. Dúchruach marks the position of Kylemore. Cnoc na hUilleann and Binn Bhriocáin are closer to hand. Further afield are Mweelrea, Binn Gorm, Leenane Hill, Devilsmother and Mám Trasna. Across the Maum Valley lie Bunnacunneen, Lugnabrick and Benlevy. Corcóg and the recently climbed Binn Chaonaigh are seen at closer quarters.

**f** Continue along the broad, rocky crest, picking up a gravelly path on the descent. There are cushions of thrift growing on scree and broken rock on the way downhill, but

A view along the rugged ridge of the Maum Turk Mountains from the top of Binn Idir an Dá Log.

later there are also some boggy patches with grass and heather. Vague paths lead to a rocky edge overlooking Loch Mám Ochóige. Take great care at this point, especially in rain and mist. There are a couple of cairns on the rocky edge, and a decision needs to be made about whether to outflank the cliffs by walking right or left.

**g** Left is the easiest, provided that the correct line is located. There is a steep, slippery, poorly trodden path, which slants left down a small scree gully where the rock actually overhangs. It is an unmistakeable route, but it needs to be searched for with care. Another steep slope of rock and grass leads down to the left of Loch Mhám Ochóige. The water sits in a rocky bowl, and it is necessary to climb uphill a little around the rim of the rock bowl before descending towards the true gap. Even then, a grassy hump needs to be crossed, with a fence to the right, before a lower gap of decaying blanket bog is reached.

**h** Turn left to descend from the gap, walking down a steepening slope of short grass which has embedded boulders. As a fine, rock-walled valley is entered, keep to the left side of a tumbling stream. There are a few little waterfalls and the river mainly runs on a bed of bare rock. Dippers dive in and around the waterfalls. Looking across the river, note an area of 'lazy beds' where potatoes were once grown. At a lower level, drift to the left, away from the river, to avoid a wide bend and walk more directly towards a bridge, noticing the sundew, marsh violet along the way.

### D  Bun na gCroc

Bun na gCroc, which translates as the Foot of the Hill, is the name of the Gaeltacht, or Irish speaking area, which encompasses all the little farmsteads between the Maum Turk Mountains and Cnoc Lios Uachtair.

i   Turn left to follow the narrow minor road over a gentle rise, passing a handful of houses, all to the left of the road, at Doire Bhó Riada. The road, which is part of the Western Way, rises again. Continue along the road, passing more farms and houses, again all to the left, at Doire Bhéal an Mháma. The road then rises gently to return to the car park at the foot of Máméan.

Loch Mhám Ochóige sits above the rugged gap of Mám Ochóige. Great care is needed on the descent to it.

# CNOC NA gCORR AND GLEANN GLAISE

**START/FINISH:**
At the road junction at An Ráithe, car parking is limited on all the approach roads. A new, wide bridge close to the junction offers the best parking option.

**DISTANCE:** 10 miles (16km).

**APPROXIMATE TIME:**
5 hours.

**HIGHEST POINT:**
1436ft (435m) on the summit of Na Cnocáin Bhána.

**MAPS:** Harveys Superwalker Connemara; OS Sheets 37 & 38.

**REFRESHMENTS:**
None actually on the route. The nearest pubs are Brennans at Béal Átha na mBreac and Keane's at Mám.

**ADVICE:**
A fairly straightforward ridge walk, suitable for times when the cloud base is lower, but a good walk in its own right. There are some fences to be crossed, but these are not difficult.

Some small hills can appear very rough and aggressive. Cnoc na gCorr has an impressive array of cliffs piled high at its eastern end, so that in some views it seems to rival the higher Maum Turk Mountains: it is an illusion. The hill is a fine introduction to a straightforward ridge walk taking in Na Cnocáin Bhána. This middle-level hill walk can be concluded by walking through Gleann Glaise, making a pleasant circuit on a good day, or a good alternative to a high-level walk when the cloud is low. The last wolf in Connemara is supposed to have been slain in Gleann Glaise.

**a** It may be possible to park a car beside an open stretch of the road running into Gleann Glaise. For the sake of having a starting point for the walk, the road junction at An Ráithe is offered, at 925543, with parking on the new bridge. This is also the point on the route closest to the occasional bus service through the Maum Valley. Roads from the Maum Valley which are signposted for Máméan offer access to the area. Follow the minor road uphill from An Ráithe to An Chorr. This road passes a small sawmill, then there is an RTE mast at a higher level, before a slight descent leads to a junction where tall fuschia bushes show.

**b** Turn right, as signposted for the Western Way. There is also a signpost indicating the way to Máméan. There are trees beside the road as it rises, then a more open stretch enclosed

A solitary hawthorn thrives on a mossy outcrop of limestone on the steep slopes of Cnoc na gCorr.

by fencing. Go through a gate on the right, but keep well to the left of the rugged cliffs on Cnoc na gCorr, passing the odd rabbit along the way.

A view across the Maum Valley from the gap of Mám Gamhna in between the two summits.

**c** A path, which is vague in places, runs up through a small valley covered in short green grass. The underlying rock is a strangely fluted limestone and there are sink holes all along the floor of the valley. 'Lazy beds', where potatoes were once grown, are also quite prominent along the valley. Look up to the right to spot a solitary hawthorn tree with a broad crown. It is rooted in a mossy outcrop of limestone, surrounded by bracken. Its branches are hoary with lichen, is watered by a tiny stream and was once even regarded as a 'fairy thorn'.

**d** Turn right to commence the ascent of Cnoc na gCorr. Keep to the steep slopes of grass, and avoid the bracken or rocky parts. A fence is reached on the boggy crest of the hill. Turning right allows for a fine view along the Maum Valley, retracing steps afterwards. Turning left allows the route to be continued immediately.

**A    Cnoc na gCorr 926533**
Anglicised as Knocknagur, Cnoc na gCorr is the Hill of the

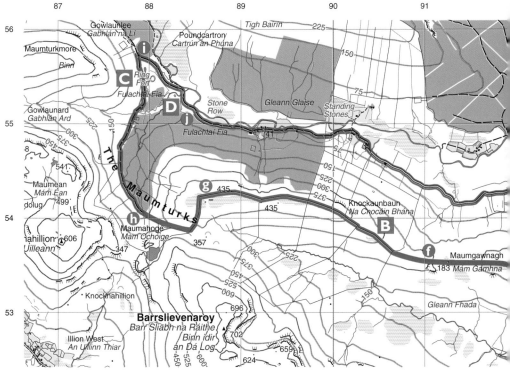

Hump. Its rugged eastern end features Aill na gCat, or the Cliff of the Cat, probably from having once had a population of wild cats. The summit ridge of Cnoc na gCorr peaks at 1020ft (310m) and there are fine views along the Maum Valley towards Lough Corrib.

**e**  Follow the fence roughly westwards along the crest of Cnoc na gCorr. Another fence needs to be crossed at a junction, then, later, the fence turns suddenly to the right. Keep walking straight onwards, away from the corner, to descend a slope of grass, bog and rocky ribs. The gap of Mám Gamhna is mostly boggy and covered in tussocky grass, but there is one hummocky area of short green grass, suggesting a limestone bedrock again. One deep bog-hole has been fenced to prevent animals straying into it.

**f**  Climb straight uphill on a grassy slope, avoiding rock, to reach three rugged little switchback tops. Cross a fence at a junction, then keep to the left side of the fence running up a broad, boggy, grassy crest. After passing a stony area, the fence veers off to the right, avoding another area of limestone

sink holes and another fenced bog-hole. Continue along the crest, walking on blanket bog and low rock outcrops. There is a short, steep climb to a small cairn, then a rocky ridge continues, bearing a vague path. Cross another fence at a junction and keep left of the fence on the next ascent. A broad, grassy crest is crossed on Na Cnocáin Bhána.

### B   Na Cnocáin Bhána 889543

Anglicised as Knockaunbaun, Na Cnocáin Bhána translates as the White Hills. The northern slopes are clothed in a young forest plantation, while the slopes facing the Maum Turk Mountains are grassy. The summit rises to 1436ft (435m). Views are necessarily limited by the proximity of so many higher mountains, but the view along the Maum Valley and Gleann Glaise is good.

**g**   Follow the fence off Na Cnocáin Bhána, drifting to the left to descend into a steep-sided grassy valley. Cross the fence and follow a stream as it tumbles downhill. There are some fine little waterfalls along its course. The stream runs beside a young forest plantation, and the grass can be quite tussocky. By crossing the stream later the end of a prominent track can be gained.

**h**  Follow the stony track gently downhill across a slope far below the gap of Mám Ochóige and Cnoc na hUilleann. Go through a gate and continue downhill along the track. Cross a stream flowing down from Binn Bhriocáin, noting a series of

A low-slung rainbow strikes the grassy crest of Na Cnocáin Bhána during a shower of rain.

ruins just downstream. Not long before the hillside track joins the main track serving Gleann Glaise there is a fine circular ring fort to the right which is worth inspecting.

### C  The Ring Fort 880555
Ring forts are circular earthern constructions which once had wooden or wattle palisades around them. There are thousands of examples across Ireland, and they were basically defended farmsteads housing extended family groups. They were used from the Iron Age into early Christian times. The one couched between the two tracks in Gleann Glaise is a fine example.

**i**  Turn right to follow the track through Gleann Glaise. Note the broad meanders of the river, which flows along a broad, rushy floor. The track has been cut from deep glacial drift, which can be studied in detail. Some parts have provided an anchor for mosses, liverworts and spleenworts, while foxgloves thrive in the disturbed ground alongside. The track crosses a concrete slab bridge, then rises. When it falls, look out for a small heap of burnt stones, partially grassed over, marking the site of a *fulachta fia* to the right. They date to c.1000BC, as does the white quartz stone row and stone pair visible from this stretch of road.

### D  Fulachta Fia 886550

A *fulachta fia* is a 'wilderness cooking place', and a measure of the ingenuity of wandering prehistoric huntsmen. Pits were dug in wet ground and lined with stone or timber, creating a water-filled trough. A fire was lit alongside and stones were heated in it. The stones were dropped into the pit, where they brought the water to a vigorous boil, so that animals such as deer or boar could be cooked. The burnt, shattered stones were raked out into heaps alongside. There are other examples nearby, but these are less easy to distinguish.

**j**   Continue following the track alongside the young forest, then look out for two large bog pine roots which have been left to the side of the track. Pass farm buildings, then pass another building and cross a cattle grid. There is a downhill stretch, followed by a climb past more farm buildings surrounded by trees. One garden contains fuchsia and hydrangea. Continuing uphill, the track becomes a narrow tarmac road and passes a solitary house surrounded by a conifer screen. The road runs across a bog featuring tussocky grass and bog myrtle, with masses of gorse appearing before the next farm. The road soon reaches the junction at An Ráithe where this route description started.

The gentle grassy crest of Na Cnocáin Bhána is seen beyond the rugged recesses of Mám Ochóige.

# CORCÓG AND BINN MHÓR FROM MÁM

**START/FINISH:**
Keane's Bar at Mám, at the junction of the R336 and R339 roads. With the aid of lifts, the road walking could be cut to a minimum, giving the option of starting high on the R336, halfway to Maam Cross, finishing on the road below Máméan.

**DISTANCE:** 12½ miles (20km).

**APPROXIMATE TIME:**
7 hours.

**HIGHEST POINT:**
2174ft (661m) on the summit of Binn Mhór.

**MAPS:**
Harveys Superwalker Connemara; OS Sheets 37, 38, 44 & 45.

**REFRESHMENTS:**
Keane's Bar at Mám.

**ADVICE:**
By cutting out the road walking, the route can be virtually halved. The mountainous stretch needs special care in mist, and the steep slopes need great care at all times as they are often wet and slippery.

At the eastern end of the Maum Turk Mountains there are three rugged summits which can be linked in a fairly straightforward walk. Clear weather is most helpful, as there are steep and rocky slopes and few trodden paths. If Ordnance Survey maps are being used, a total of four are needed to cover the whole walk, while Harveys have the whole route on one sheet! The circuit is described from Mám, and with assistance from a motoring friend the road walking at the beginning and end can be omitted. The route described includes a stretch of the waymarked Western Way as well as the Patrician pilgrimage route over the gap of Máméan.

**A    Mám 965528**
Also known as Maum or Maum Bridge, with Keane's Bar facing the bridge. Originally, the bar was called the Corrib Lodge. It was built by Alexander Nimmo, a Scottish engineer, who also built fine stone bridges throughout the region. There is easy access from the river to Lough Corrib. In the past lake steamers from Galway used to visit Mám and moor at the bridge.

**a**    Starting from Keane's Bar, cross the river and follow the R336 road southwards in the direction of Maam Cross. The road leads across a bog, then passes a few buildings, Note the Western Way signposts pointing to right and left, either side of Teernakill Bridge. The road begins to rise across a broad and boggy slope, with the mountain slopes of Corcóg to the right

Looking across the mountainsides from a prow of rock, with Mullach Glas seen in the background.

and solitary Leic Aimhréidh to the left. Some turf cuttings can be spotted beside the road on the way up to a broad gap. It is helpful if a lift can be arranged for this first stretch, so that the walk can start straight away with an ascent of Corcóg.

**b**    There are a couple of small parking spaces to the right near the top of the road. Head off to the right from either of them, picking a way across the lower boggy slopes to reach the steep and rugged slopes of Corcóg. There is no real path, so choose any course which leads uphill on grass and heather, avoiding numerous rocky outcrops. Take a close look at some of the rock faces, which support a range of plants: holly, St. Patrick's cabbage, spleenwort, butterwort, mosses and ferns. The ground gets steeper and rockier with height, and hands might need to be used in some places. In mist, drifting to the left will lead towards the line of a fence, which offers a sure guide uphill. The whole summit area of Corcóg is hummocky rock, heather and grass, crossed by a line of old fenceposts, sparse in places, without any wire between them.

## B    Corcóg 952492
The Ordnance Survey used to label this mountain as Leckavrea, then called it Corcogemore, and currently leave it nameless. Corcóg translates as  Beehive, which seems to allude to its shape. Roderick O'Flaherty wrote of 'the mountains of Corcoga, in the confines of Balynahynsy, Ross, and Moycullin countreys, where the fat deere is frequently hunted.' There is a cairn on top at an altitude of 2012ft (609m).

A statue of St. Patrick stands in front of the cave known as St. Patrick's Bed at the gap of Máméan.

**c**    The fenceposts can be followed down to the next gap in mist, but in clear weather it may be better to stay high on the shoulder of the mountain before dropping down to the gap. Either way, there are rock outcrops, boulders, boggy bits and stony patches to cross. The gap is heathery and peppered with boulders. The line of fenceposts lead up a bouldery slope, passing behind a rocky peak above the gap. The little peak is known as Crúiscín, or the Little Jug. There is a clear path climbing steeply uphill following the old fenceposts. The ground is rocky in places, but when the gradient eases the path is either peaty or gravelly. The summit of Mullach Glas is a hummocky area of rocky outcrops, abundantly scattered with stones and small pools, that provide a suitable habitat for bilberry, crowberry and clubmoss.

## C    Mullach Glas 937493
Mullach Glas can be translated as a Green Top or a Grey Top.

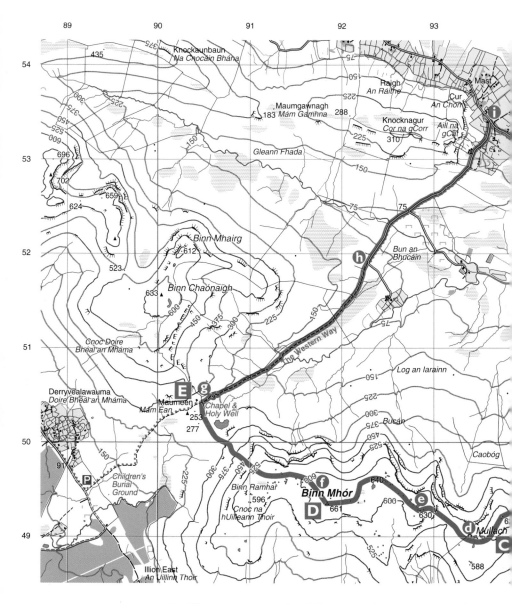

In different seasons and in different weather conditions, either could be appropriate. The summit rises to 2045ft (622m).

**d** Keep to the rocky crest of Mullach Glas after leaving the summit cairn. There are bright splashes of white quartz in the quartzite rock, and a sizeable pool should be noticed. A wire

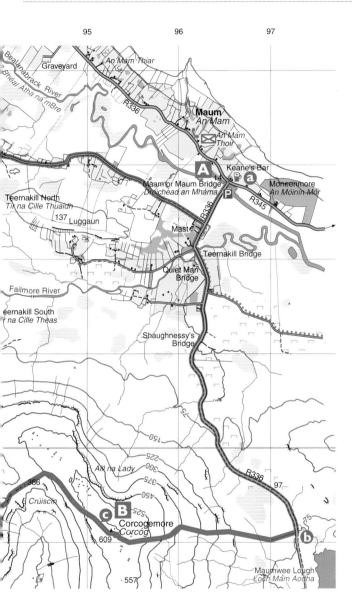

fence rises over the ridge and needs to be crossed. Walk down a stony slope to reach the next gap, which bears a cairn.

**e**   Climb uphill from the gap, keeping to the left of a crag, walking on grass, heather and boulders. The ascent is not as difficult as those already endured, and there is a cairn at the top

A dripping natural limestone grotto beside the Western Way features an abundance of ferns.

to confirm the correct course. This is not the true summit of Binn Mhór, so continue walking along the broad, rocky, hummocky crest, crossing a little gap. Gradually rise across more of the same terrain to reach a trig point marking the true summit. There is a small, circular drystone shelter just before this point.

### D   Binn Mhór 918494

Binn Mhór is simply the Big Mountain, and the highest point reached on this walk, at 2174ft (661m). There are views of the Twelve Bens from Binn Leitrí to Maolan, then Dúchruach and Maolchnoc are seen. The middle section of the Maum Turk Mountains gives way to Mweelrea and Leenane Hill. Binn Gorm, Sheefry Hills and Devilsmother are noted, along with Bunnacunneen, Mám Trasna, Lugnabrick and Benlevy. After Mullach Glas there is a broad sweep of lake-strewn bogland, an indented coastline and low hills including Cashel Hill and Errisbeg.

**f**   A rocky ridge leads downhill at a reasonable angle and should pose no difficulties at first. However, there is a much steeper and rougher descent to the gap of Máméan. Broken rock, hidden benches of rock, slippery wet areas and stones which move when trodden upon make this an awkward, and potentially dangeropus descent. Keep an eye trained on the little lough at the gap, aiming for its left side, but if difficulties are encountered, then try drifting further to the right and find a fence which reveals an easier course down to the waterside. Cross the hummocky, boggy gap to reach a fairly well trodden track near the pilgrimage site of Máméan.

### E   Máméan 905504

Máméan is Anglicised as Maumeen and means the Pass of the Birds. Roderick O'Flaherty wrote of the place: 'At Mamen, there springs out of a stone a litle water, named from St. Patrick, which is a present remedy against murrein in cattel, not only applyed, but alsoe as soon as tis sent for they begin to have ease.' The pilgrimage site features a small chapel called Cillín Phádraig; a covered altar called Carraig Aifrinn Phádraig Naofa; Leaba Phádraig, or St. Patrick's Bed; Tobar Phádraig, or St. Patrick's Well; Buntobar Phádraig Naofa, another holy well; a statue inscribed Pádraig Mór na hÉireann; and the Stations of the Cross in a wide anti-clockwise circuit around the site. Note the Connemara Marble on the altar and the lovely collection of ferns growing behind it. It is said that St. Patrick reached the summit of the pass, but did not cross it. Instead, he blessed the outlying regions of Connemara from it. The pilgrimage had been abandoned, but has been revived in recent years, as the dedication dates on the various structures attest, running from 1980–93.

**g** Cross a stile beside a gate in a fence close to the pilgrimage site. At first, the rough pilgrimage track crosses bare rock, then it steps down onto a grassy surface. The track passes strangely worn limestone outcrops, full of sink holes, and home to a variety of plants, including hawthorn, St. Patrick's cabbage, ivy, wood sorrel, spleenwort, ferns and mosses. A couple of streams need to be forded, but others are culverted or bridged. There are two other stiles beside gates on the gentle descent, with occasional Western Way marker posts bearing yellow arrows. Please note that much of this section of the route may have suffered flood damage.

**h** The track joins a narrow, patchy tarmac road, where some walkers might be able to arrange to be collected. If continuing on foot, then walk down to a concrete bridge over the river in Gleann Fhada. The road climbs uphill, over a rise in the shadow of the craggy Aill na gCat, or the Cliff of the Cat, then continues downhill passing a couple of houses.

**i** Turn right at a road junction, as signposted for the Western Way. The road has an unruly series of hedgerows. Holly, alder, hawthorn, gorse, rhododendron, fuchsia, firs, pines, and foxgloves mark the route. Most of the land alongside is boggy, though there are a few small fields. There are some houses along the road, as well as a small, recent roadside memorial. The last features are the Garda Barracks and a GAA sports pitch surrounded by scots pines. Turn left at the end of the An Mhama road to head straight back to Keane's Bar.

Corcóg and Mullach Glas as seen from the Western Way on the long walk back to Keane's Bar at Mám.

# CORCÓG AND BINN MHÓR FROM MAAM CROSS

**START/FINISH:**
Maam Cross, at the junction of the main N59 and the R336 road, often referred to as the 'Piccadilly of Connemara'.

**DISTANCE:** 16 miles (26km).

**APPROXIMATE TIME:** 9 hours.

**HIGHEST POINT:** 2174ft (661m) on the summit of Binn Mhór.

**MAPS:** Harveys Superwalker Connemara; OS Sheets 37, 44 & 45.

**REFRESHMENTS:**
The only refreshments on the route are at Peacocke's Hotel and Viewing Tower.

**ADVICE:**
This is a long and tough walk. The mountain walk is fairly straightforward, but the descent to Máméan needs care. If a lift cannot be arranged at the foot of Máméan, then there is a long, low-level walk along tracks to bring the circuit back to a close.

Maam Cross is small in stature, originally no more than a handful of buildings, and now the site of a recently-built hotel complex; it is one of Connemara's major crossroads. Mr. A. J. H. Peacocke opened a bar on the crossroads in 1888. The Irish name of An Teach Deoite means the Burning House, as the place has been twice burnt. *The Quiet Man*, starring John Wayne and Maureen O'Hara, was filmed around Cong in 1950 and a replica cottage from the film, built beside Peacocke's, now serves as a museum. In February the Annual Bogman's Ball is held; barrows of turf are burnt and steaks are cooked on shovels. On the last Tuesday in October there is the Maam Cross Big Fair, with Connemara Ponies being bought and sold, as well as other livestock, farm machinery and almost any other saleable items! The Big Fair brings the crossroads almost to a standstill.

**A   Maam Cross 976462**
**a**   Start from Peacocke's Hotel at Maam Cross and follow the road signposted for Mám. Note the old railway station and platform away to the right, and a derelict railway cottage and a more recent house to the left. Continue along the road, passing a green corrugated hut beside a lough. The road runs across a broad and bleak bog, passing turf cuttings and another lough. There are a couple of tracks to the left as the road rises to a broad gap, and the moorland to the left is also fenced. When the fence suddenly turns left across the bog, the ascent of Corcóg can begin. It is a good idea to arrange for a lift up the road if possible, so that the ascent of Corcóg can begin in earnest.

A statue of St. Patrick at the gap of Máméan looks towards Binn Mhór, whose steep slopes need special care.

**b**   There is a small parking space on the left near the top of the road. Head off to the left, picking a way across the lower boggy slopes to reach the steep and rugged slopes of Corcóg – spot the butterwort. There is no real path, so choose any course which leads uphill on grass and heather, or follow the line of the fence, avoiding numerous rocky outcrops. Take a close look at some of the rock faces, which support a range of plants: holly, St. Patrick's cabbage, spleenwort, mosses, ferns. The ground gets steeper and rockier with height, and hands might need to be used in some places. In mist, the line of the fence offers a sure guide uphill. The whole summit area of Corcóg is hummocky rock, heather and grass, crossed by a line of old fenceposts without any wire between them.

A small chapel and altar have been constructed for pilgrims at Máméan, dedicated to St. Patrick.

## B   Corcóg 952492

The Ordnance Survey used to label this mountain as Leckavrea, then called it Corcogemore, and currently leave it nameless. Corcóg translates as Beehive, which seems to allude to its shape. Roderick O'Flaherty wrote of 'the mountains of Corcoga, in the confines of Balynahynsy, Ross, and Moycullin countreys, where the fat deere is frequently hunted.' There is a cairn on top at an altitude of 2012ft (609m).

**c**   The fenceposts can be followed down to the next gap in mist, but in clear weather it may be better to stay high on the shoulder of the mountain before dropping down to the gap. Either way, there are rock outcrops, boulders, boggy bits and stony patches to cross. The gap is heathery and peppered with boulders. The line of fenceposts lead up a bouldery slope, passing behind a rocky peak above the gap. The little peak is known as Crúiscín, or the Little Jug. There is a clear path climbing steeply uphill following the old fenceposts. The ground

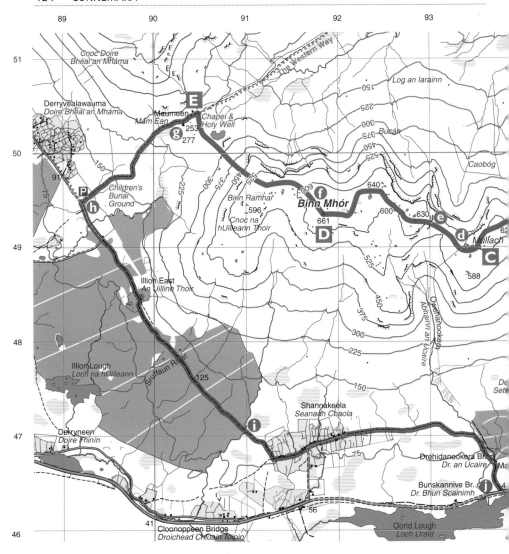

is rocky in places, but when the gradient eases the path is either peaty or gravelly. The summit of Mullach Glas is a hummocky area of rocky outcrops, abundantly scattered with stones and small pools, providing an ideal habitat for bilberry, crowberry, and clubmoss.

### C  Mullach Glas 937493

Mullach Glas is translated as either a Green Top or a Grey Top. In different seasons and weather conditions, either could be appropriate. The summit rises to 2045ft (622m).

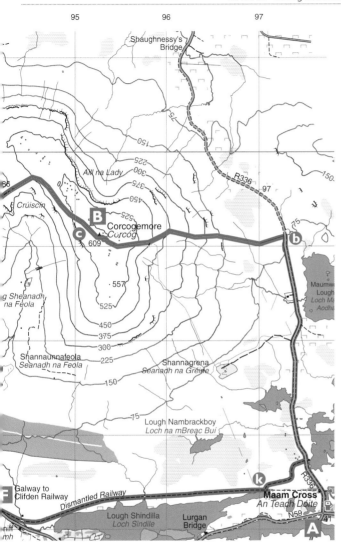

**d** Keep to the rocky crest of Mullach Glas after leaving the summit cairn. There are bright splashes of white quartz in the quartzite rock, and a sizeable pool should be noticed. A wire fence rises over the ridge and needs to be crossed. Walk down a stony slope to reach the next gap, which bears a cairn.

**e** Climb uphill from the gap, keeping to the left of a crag, walking on grass, heather and boulders. The ascent is not as difficult as those already endured, and there is a cairn at the top to confirm the correct course. This is not the true summit of

Binn Mhór, so continue walking along the broad, rocky, hummocky crest, crossing a little gap. Gradually rise across more of the same terrain to reach a trig point marking the true summit. There is a small, circular drystone shelter just before this point.

### D   Binn Mhór 918494

Binn Mhór is simply the Big Mountain, and the highest point reached on this walk, at 2174ft (661m). There are views of the Twelve Bens from Binn Leitrí to Maolan, then Dúchruach and Maolchnoc are seen. The middle section of the Maum Turk Mountains gives way to Mweelrea and Leenane Hill. Binn Gorm, Sheefry Hills and Devilsmother are noted, along with Bunnacunneen, Mám Trasna, Lugnabrick and Benlevy. After Mullach Glas there is a broad sweep of lake-strewn bogland, an indented coastline and low hills including Cashel Hill and Errisbeg.

**f**   A rocky ridge leads downhill at a reasonable angle and should pose no difficulties at first. However, there is a much steeper and rougher descent to the gap of Máméan. Broken rock, hidden benches of rock, slippery wet areas and stones which move when trodden upon make this an awkward descent. Keep an eye trained on the little lough on the gap, aiming for its left side, but if difficulties are encountered, then try drifting further to the right and find a fence which reveals an easier course down to the waterside. Cross the hummocky, boggy gap to reach a fairly well trodden track near the pilgrimage site of Máméan.

Parts of the pilgrim path leading away from Máméan cross bare rock. Other parts are stony or grassy.

**E    Máméan 905504**

Máméan is Anglicised as Maumeen and means the Pass of the Birds. Roderick O'Flaherty wrote of the place: 'At Mam-en, there springs out of a stone a litle water, named from St. Patrick, which is a present remedy against murrein in cattel, not only applyed, but alsoe as soon as tis sent for they begin to have ease.' The pilgrimage site features a small chapel called Cillín Phádraig; a covered altar called Carraig Aifrinn Phádraig Naofa; Leaba Phádraig, or St. Patrick's Bed; Tobar Phádraig, or St. Patrick's Well; Buntobar Phádraig Naofa, another holy well; a statue inscribed Pádraig Mór na hÉireann; and the Stations of the Cross in a wide anti-clockwise circuit around the site. Note the Connemara Marble on the altar and the lovely collection of ferns growing behind it. It is said that St. Patrick reached the summit of the pass, but did not cross it. Instead, he blessed the outlying regions of Connemara from it. The pilgrimage had been abandoned, but has been revived in recent years, as the dedication dates on the various structures attest, running from 1980–93.

**g**    Turn left along the track to leave Máméan. The track runs across bare rock for a while, with other parts being stony or grassy, often flanked by kerbstones and violets growing. There is a stream to cross at a lower level, and a sad children's burial ground 220 yards (200m) to the southeast, just below a long bush, and there is a stile beside a gate in a fence. The track runs down to a car park beside a minor road. There is the opportunity to be collected at this point by arrangement, but there are also a low-level series of tracks which can be linked to lead back to Maam Cross.

**h**    Turn left along the road, passing a stand of forest to reach a small building on a road bend. Just to the right, at the corner of a forest, are a few eucalyptus trees, which actually grow quite well in bleak and barren parts of Connemara. Go over a stile beside a gate at the road corner, following a clear track into the forest. The track crosses a stream and later passes some old enclosures at Illion West; the remains of an old farmstead. A few deciduous trees are located in the forest in this area. The track undulates across the slope and there are some unplanted areas with views of the mountain slopes. There are a few streams to cross, then a wider river needs to be crossed beyond the forest gate. Note that this can be a powerful flow after heavy rain.

**i**    A grassy, muddy track leads away from the river, alongside a fence, turning right down a slope to pass some old enclosures. Turn left along a muddy track and pass through a gate beside a

Turf-cutting machinery and tractors adapted for work on soft bogs could be seen on the way to Maam Cross.

farm. Follow the farm access track, passing through another gate, crossing a bridge over a tumbling stream and continuing along a narrow tarmac road to a junction. Continue straight onwards, following the road gradually uphill past a few houses and enclosed fenced or walled fields. Go through a gate after the end of the tarmac, following a track gradually downhill with a fence to the right. After having passed through a gate there is a fence to the left. Later, the track, which can be wet in places, drifts to the right across open bogland to reach a river at the edge of a forest, here you will see a large mobile phone mast. Cross a bridge over the river and follow a clear track down to the main N59 road. Along the way, note the purple moor grass and bog myrtle.

**j**  Turn left along the main road, then left again where an old railway trackbed drops into a rock cutting. This line is usually wet and muddy, in which case keep to the upper edge of the cutting, on the right, to reach a bridge over a river. Holly, hawthorn and gorse are a distinctive feature. A grassy embankment becomes lined with trees, then there is a wet and muddy stretch. There are views across Loch Sindile, with its wooded island. Mallard and swans make this their home. Cross a fence on a bridge, then follow the embankment towards another cutting. Again, a wet and muddy stretch can be avoided by keeping to the right of the cutting. Another grassy stretch of the trackbed is lined by trees and bushes: willow, birch, hawthorn, holly and bramble.

### F  Galway to Clifden Railway 834476
Snaking alongside the main road, then cutting across extensive bogs, the Galway to Clifden Railway was a part of the Midland Great Western Railway Company. The construction was grant-aided to provide employment during a time of great need, and the line was officially opened in 1895. The Connemara stations were at Oughterard, Maam Cross, Recess and Ballynahinch, with the terminus at Clifden. Trains ceased running along the line in 1935 and in 1936 the track was lifted.

**k**  The last part of the trackbed is blocked by gorse, but there is an exit to the left along a bog road, passing turf cuttings. Turf cutting machinery could be inspected along the way. Tractors have double or even triple wheels to gain purchase on the bog surface. Other machines have caterpillar tracks, cutting blades, scoops and conveyor belt systems. Follow the bog road to reach the R336 road, then turn right to return to Maam Cross.

# RECESS AND CNOC LIOS UACHTAIR

Cnoc Lios Uachtair is a hill of no great height, but it seems to be as rugged as the higher mountains which surround it. Positioned as it is between the Twelve Bens and the Maum Turk Mountains: there are fine views of both ranges. The walk over Cnoc Lios Uachtair can be conveniently based on the straggly village of Recess. The colourful facade of Joyce's General Stores, and its associated businesses, are well telegraphed both ways along the main road, and there is ample car parking available overlooking Loch Gleann Dá Loch.

**A   Joyce's of Recess 846477**
Recess takes its name from the Recess Hotel, which became the Railway Hotel, but was burnt down in the 'Troubles' in 1922. The Irish name for the village is Srath Salach, meaning the Riverside Meadow of Willows. There is no real centre, but tourism centres on Joyce's General Store, Joyce's Craft Shop and Paddy Festy's Bar and Restaurant. Amusing signs point out that items for sale include 'Beer, Books, Eggs, Marble, Wool' and services include 'Filling Station, Undertaker' and another sign promises 'For those of you who like this sort of place, this is the sort of place you like'. Across the road is a curious triangular lakeside monument stating that 'On This Site in 1897 Nothing Happened'!

**a**   Follow the main N59 road away from Joyce's General Stores in the direction of Maam Cross. The road runs beside Loch Gleann Dá Loch, which has a wooded shore, with alder, birch, oak, holly, willow, sycamore, rhododendron, gorse and bramble

**START/FINISH:**
At Joyce's General Stores in Recess, on the main N59 road between Maam Cross and Clifden.

**DISTANCE:** 6 miles (9.5km).

**APPROXIMATE TIME:**
3 hours.

**HIGHEST POINT:**
1314ft (401m) on the summit of Cnoc Lios Uachtair.

**MAPS:** Harveys Superwalker Connemara; OS Sheet 44.

**REFRESHMENTS:**
Paddy Festy's Bar and Restaurant is located at the start/finish of the walk beside Joyce's General Stores.

**ADVICE:**
Don't be tempted to follow too much of the old Galway to Clifden railway line, as some parts are very overgrown. The hill walk is essentially quite straightforward, though care is needed to choose the correct line of descent in mist.

Joyce's General Stores at Recess – part of a complex catering for the needs of tourists on the main road.

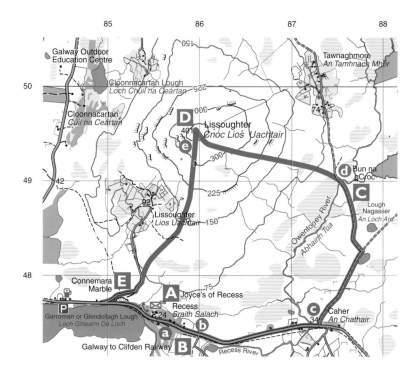

growing. The road has been widened to include the trackbed of the old Galway to Clifden Railway, but when passing a quarry and the Post Office, the trackbed pursues a course parallel to the main road and may be followed for a short while. When a red corrugated building is reached on a former railway platform, switch back to the main road to avoid a swampy, overgrown cutting.

### B  Galway to Clifden Railway 855475
Snaking alongside the main road, the Galway to Clifden Railway was a part of the Midland Great Western Railway Company. The construction was grant-aided to provide employment during a time of great need, and the line was officially opened in 1895. The Connemara stations were at Oughterard, Maam Cross, Recess and Ballynahinch, with the terminus at Clifden. Trains ceased running along the line in 1935 and in 1936 the track was lifted.

**b**  Follow the main road over a rise, passing the Garda Station and a school. Again, there is a short stretch of the old railway

A view across Bun na gCroc, the Gaeltacht, or Irish speaking area, between Cnoc Lios Uachtair and the Maum Turks.

trackbed which can be followed beside the road, but this too becomes overgrown by gorse and cut by fencing within a short while. Follow the main road past a couple of houses hidden behind screens of conifers, then cross a broad bogland to reach the Catholic church of Teampuill Phádraig. Cross the river beyond, then turn left along a narrow minor road signposted for Mámméan.

c   The minor road is mostly founded on rock, but is entirely surrounded by extensive blanket bog. Pass a stone tablet which reads Bun na gCroc, then, later, cross a bridge over a stream. The road rises to a small, reedy lough, where there is a left turn along an even narrower road. There is a sweeping view across the broad bogland, with Cnoc Lios Uachtair rising ahead. The road passes a small quarry in a bank of glacial drift, then descends to cross a bridge over a river.

### C   Bun na gCroc
Bun na gCroc, which translates as the Foot of the Hill, is the name of the Gaeltacht, or Irish speaking area, which encompasses all the little farmsteads between the Maum Turk Mountains and Cnoc Lios Uachtair.

d   After crossing the bridge, follow the road a short way, then step over a low part of the fence to the left. Walk straight up the slopes of Cnoc Lios Uachtair, first crossing a slope where most of the bog has been cut for turf. The resultant surface is uneven and stony. At a higher level there is a boggy terrace, then a firmer grass and heather slope with a few embedded boulders.

The dark form of Cnoc Lios Uachtair seen from the bright ridge of Eochair in the Twelve Bens.

Note the 'lazy beds' to the left, where potatoes were once grown. This patch of former cultivated land on the rugged hillside bears the name of Garraí na Sceiche, or the Thorn Garden. The slope steepens and features rock slabs, then the upper parts of the hill are rocky, stony, hummocky, heathery and boggy. There is a fence zig-zagging across the top, and the summit cairn lies just above a junction of fences.

### D   Cnoc Lios Uachtair 859495

Anglicised as Lissoughter, Cnoc Lios Uachtair means the Hill of the Upper Fort, though if there was a fort in the area, it was destroyed long ago. There is an extensive view, but the Twelve Bens and Maum Turk Mountains are of particular interest. Look around to spot Cashel Hill, Errisbeg, Derryclare Lough, Binn Leitrí, Binn Gabhar, Binn Dhoire Chláir, Binn Chorr, Binn an Choire Bhig, Maolchnoc, Mweelrea, Binn Bhriocáin, Cnoc na hUilleann, Binn Idir an Dá Log, Binn Chaonaigh, Mámean and Binn Mhór. The summit of Cnoc Lios Uachtair rises to 1314ft (401m). This is a good point from which to study the layout of a number of walks in the Twelve Bens, Maum Turk Mountains, and in the lower valleys around the lakes.

**e** Cross back over the fence to start the descent. Start by walking roughly southwards down a rough, rocky and boggy slope. At a lower level, a gentle slope of short-grassed bog proves easier to descend. This bog is drained by a small stream which has been tapped by a long hosepipe. The idea is to walk towards Loch Gleann Dá Loch, drifting a little to the right to hit a narrow road. Turn left along the road, passing above a quarry and running down to the main N59 road. A right turn along the main road, or along the wooded shore of Loch Gleann Dá Loch leads straight back to Joyce's General Stores.

A distant view showing solitary Cnoc Lios Uachtair beyond the shining levels of Lough Inagh.

### E   Connemara Marble

Connemara Marble was first quarried at Recess in the 1820s. The enterprise was started by Thomas Martin of Ballynahinch Castle. King Edward VII and Queen Alexandra visited the quarry during their tour of Connemara in 1903. The marble appears as a variable band in highly contorted strata, often proving difficult to locate and exploit at times. Connemara Marble is worked at a marble factory beside the main road at Recess, then sold in the craft shop alongside Joyce's General Stores.

# CIRCUIT OF DERRYCLARE LOUGH

**START/FINISH:**
Canal Stage, where parking is available beside the bridge on the main N59 road between Clifden and Recess, close to the junction with the R341 road.

**DISTANCE:** 8 miles (13km).

**APPROXIMATE TIME:**
4½ hours.

**HIGHEST POINT:**
165ft (50m) on the lower slopes of Binn Dhoire Chláir towards the end of the walk.

**MAPS:** Harveys Superwalker Connemara; OS Sheets 37 & 44.

**REFRESHMENTS:**
Inagh Valley Inn.

**ADVICE:**
Almost three-quarters of this walk is easy, and mostly on firm, dry surfaces. The final stretch, however, is quite rugged, crossing clear-felled forest terrain, following a rugged forest ride and traversing a pathless boggy slope.

It is possible to walk most of the way around Derryclare Lough using roads, forest tracks and a disused railway trackbed. However, that still leaves an awkward link along a rugged forest ride and across a bleak and boggy slope. The route description is structured to start and finish at Canal Stage, on the main N59 road, so that the toughest stretch is covered last. The Inagh Valley Inn appears at roughly the halfway point, and for those walkers who do not wish to complete the full circuit, the inn is a handy place to arrange to be collected. Keep an eye peeled on this walk as rare pine martens have been observed in the area.

### A    Canal Stage 803475

Canal Stage obtains its name partly from the canalisation of the river and partly from the fact that it was a stage on the Bianconi coach transport service early in the 19th Century. The name is still in use by both the Connemara Bus and Bus Éireann drivers. The bridge divides the Upper Ballynahinch Fishery from the Lough Inagh Fishery, for permit purposes.

Looking across a reedy part of Derryclare Lough towards the shadowed form of Cnoc Lios Uachtair.

**a** There is a good parking space beside Canal Bridge. salmon, trout and otters inhabit the canal. The walk starts by following the main N59 road in the direction of Galway. The road runs close to the southern shore of Derryclare Lough and is equipped with good grass verges. There is a fine view which takes in a pine-clad island backed by the mountainous form of Binn Dhoire Chláir. When the road bends right, away from the shore, pass a cottage that is surrounded by rhododendron and fuchsia, then turn left at a former level crossing.

**b** There is a gate beside the road, leading directly onto the trackbed of the former Galway to Clifden Railway. There is an old railway cottage immediately to the right, and the trackbed is flanked by trees and bushes at first. Emerging onto a broad area of bog, the slightly raised gravel surface is lightly grassed, firm and dry. A few turf cuttings, Derryclare Lough and Binn Dhoire Chláir all lie to the left, while a forest stands to the right. There is a gate to go through, then the trackbed runs close to the shore, with a view across a large number of shrubby islets and rocks, with the Maum

Looking across a pine-clad island in Derryclare Lough to the mountain of Binn Dhoire Chláir.

Turk Mountains rising beyond. Low rock cuttings are passed through, where seepage from the bog makes the surface wet and muddy. Bog myrtle and snipe are found here. There is another firm, dry, raised stretch of trackbed running parallel to a river, with a forest on the far bank. Pass a placid stretch of the river – heron habitat – then weave between the gorse bushes towards the end of the trackbed. There is a gate leading to a house hidden in a clump of trees. Don't go through the gate, but turn right and cross over an unfenced boggy rise to reach the main N59 road again.

## B    Galway to Clifden Railway 834476
Snaking alongside the main road, then cutting across extensive bogs, the Galway to Clifden Railway was a part of the Midland Great Western Railway Company. The construction was grant-aided to provide employment during a time of need in the years

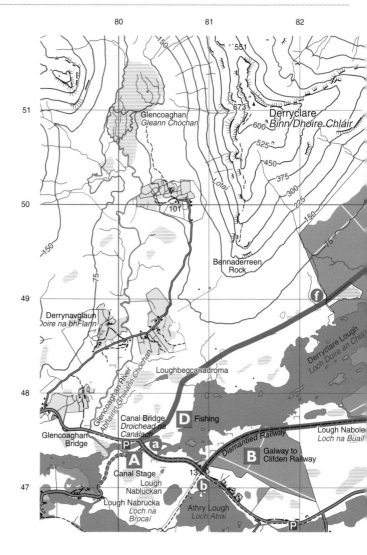

following the Great Famine, and the line was officially opened in 1895. The Connemara stations were at Oughterard, Maam Cross, Recess and Ballynahinch, with the terminus at Clifden. Trains ceased running along the line in 1935 and in 1936 the track was lifted.

c   Turn left along the road, which swings right and crosses the river at the Weir Bridge. Note the old railway bridge just upstream beside Loch Gleann Dá Loch. There is a road junction beside Recess House, with a lavish array of signposts for

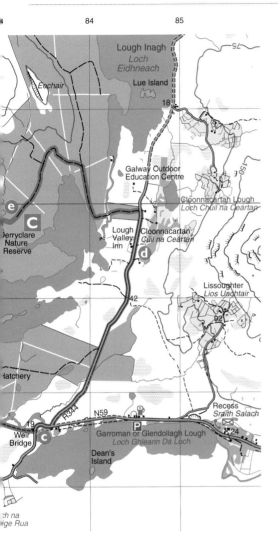

Connemara National Park and Kylemore Abbey. Turn left at this point along the R344 road, the road for Kylemore. This road crosses a bog, then rises through a forest, continuing up another boggy slope. At the top of the road, hidden in a clump of trees, is the Inagh Valley Inn offering food and drink.

**d**  The road descends, flanked with fuschia, crosses another boggy slope, then enters a stand of forestry. Turn left to cross a stile beside a gate, where a sign reads Coill Dhoire Chláir, and follow a forest track downhill, keeping a lookout for crossbills,

The walk exits from the boggy unforested strip and contours above an island-studded part of Derryclare Lough.

and siskins. The track crosses a river on two bridges, using an island as a stepping stone. There are fishery paths to right and left, but walk straight along the track, away from the river, passing a barrier gateway in the forest. There are glimpes of Derryclare Lough between the trees, but later these are lost. Turn left at a junction of tracks, then follow the track as it makes a pronounced left bend and passes a wooden hut. The track forges straight across a clear-felled and replanted area, then reaches its terminus. Note that the walk becomes very tough from here onwards.

### C   Derryclare Nature Reserve 835496

South of the end of the forest track in Derryclare Wood is a small nature reserve. It is formed of a strip of deciduous woodland along the shore of Derryclare Lough. This woodland features a variety of fungi, ferns and lichens. As well as the semi-natural woodland, which is predominantly oak, there are small ponds and lakeshore ecosystems. Since the clear-felling of the adjacent forest the woodland stands out rather more prominently. Hidden from sight are the ruins of Derryclare Lodge, which was once used by fishing parties. Access is not easy, as will be discovered!

e   Leave the end of the forest track and pick a way across a devastated slope of broken branches, hidden holes, rocks and boulders, to reach a stream beside a tall stand of forest. Follow the watercourse downstream to reach a fence at the edge of the nature reserve, and turn right. It might be best to cross the fence and follow it through a forest ride, but this means crossing it again at a corner. Continue straight along the forest ride, rising slightly on tussocky grass, squelching downhill to cross a small stream in a dip, then climbing again. The ride levels out, then there is a broad area of quaking bog, flanked by forest, to cross. Keep to the right, then step across the forest fence to gain an extensive area of bog on the lower slopes of Binn Dhoire Chláir.

**f** Continue straight across the boggy slope, aiming to stay high above the shore of Derryclare Lough. Progress should be maintained between the 30m and 50m (100ft and 160ft) contours. The way is boggy and pathless, but also gently graded and not too rocky or clothed in tussocky grass – good habitat for foxes and Irish hares. Besides, there are fine views across the lough. Keeping an eye to the ground, look out for an area of greener grass which is enclosed by low walls and shows signs of having been cleared of boulders for cultivation. By keeping high above the shore, a couple of final humps are crossed before a scant sheep path leads down to the road bridge at Canal Stage. There is a fence to be crossed to return to the parking space where the walk started.

### D Fishing

While compiling *An Irish Sketch Book* William Makepeace Thackeray commented: 'O you who laboriously throw flies in English rivers, and catch at the expiration of a day's walking, casting and wadeing two or three feeble little trout of two or three ounces in weight, how you would rejoice to have but one hour's sport on Derryclare or Ballynahinch; where you have but cast, and lo! a big trout springs to your fly.'

Cashel Hill is seen rising across a lake-spattered bogland beyond the foot of Derryclare Lough.

# CIRCUIT OF BALLYNAHINCH LOUGH

**START/FINISH:**
Ben Lettery Youth Hostel, on the main N59 road between Clifden and Recess. Parking is available on a small loop of old road crossing an old bridge just to the east of the hostel.

**DISTANCE:** 8 miles (13km).

**APPROXIMATE TIME:**
4 hours.

**HIGHEST POINT:**
Most of the circuit is around 100ft (30m).

**MAPS:** Harveys Superwalker Connemara; OS Sheet 44.

**REFRESHMENTS:**
Ballynahinch Castle has a public bar and restaurant.

**ADVICE:**
The walk along the main N59 road can be omitted entirely if the walk schedule can be tied in with local bus services.

**A**n easy circuit around Ballynahinch Lough linking roads, forest tracks and specially constructed woodland paths. The whole circuit is accomplished on firm, dry surfaces through forest and woods, or across bogs and lower mountain slopes. History and heritage abound and there are some fine views across the lough to the Twelve Bens. The stretch along the main N59 road could be omitted by using the occasional local bus services, but be sure to check the timetables in advance and structure the route accordingly. Watch carefully in the woodlands as Ballynahinch is known to be a haunt of rare pine martens.

**a** Start at the Ben Lettery Youth Hostel, following the main N59 road westwards in the direction of Clifden. The road passes a derelict building hidden in a stand of conifers on the lower slopes of Binn Leitrí. Generally, there are good views across Ballynahinch Lough, with Cashel Hill being the prominent hill beyond. The only intrusion into the scene is an ugly communications mast sited on the lower slopes of Binn Leitrí.

Looking along the shore of Ballynahinch Lough, a house stands beside the water near Ballynahinch Castle.

### A    Castle Island 763480

The ivy-clad tower house on the tiny Castle Island near the head of Ballynahinch Lough dates from 1565. It possibly replaced an earlier structure which may have been a 'crannóg', or fortified lake dwelling. Ballynahinch is the Anglicised form of Baile na hInse, which translates as the Settlement of the Island. The builder was Dónal O'Flaherty, husband of the notorious sea queen Gráinne Mhael, but it changed hands within the O'Flaherty clan as a result of almost constant feuding. 'Humanity' Dick Martin is reputed to have imprisoned tenants in the castle if he found them treating animals cruelly. The Martins also had a tea-house in the ruins of the castle and were supposed to have operated a still-house there when the family fortunes were waning.

b    Beyond the head of the lake is a minor road on the left, signposted for Ballynahinch Castle. Follow this road gently downhill, across a bridge, then uphill across a clear-felled and replanted area of forest. Oak, holly and sycamore provide holds for climbing ivy. There is a turning on the left for the Old Manor, signposted as a private residence. Follow this fenced access road gently downhill to catch a glimpse of the fine old stone building.

Walkers cross the footbridge over the Abhainn Mhór, which flow southwards from Ballynahinch Lough.

### B    The Old Manor 758478

The name is misleading. Although the building is a splendid stone structure, carefully converted to timeshare apartments, it was never a manor house. In fact it was a stable block, built in 1895. The stalls were, however, carved from the finest Connemara Marble!

c    Turn right through a small gate marked as the Castle Walk. A fine gravel path descends through delightful mossy woodlands dominated by oak and holly. There is a small clearing with a view along an enclosed portion of Ballynahinch Lough, then there is another small gate to pass through. There is a fine understorey in the woods. Note the hawthorn, rhododendron, bilberry, woodrush, wood sorrel, ferns and mosses. Bracken and brambles feature wherever there are small clearings. There is a point reached where the path divides at a stream.

### C    Church Lake 758475

A right turn at the stream leads up to a curious feature at a nearby road. An arched bridge had been dammed at some stage after its construction to raise the level of Church Lake – named after a now-lost Medieval abbey – across the road, with the water having been piped to provide power before being released into Ballynahinch Lough. If detouring to inspect this dam, return to the lakeshore path.

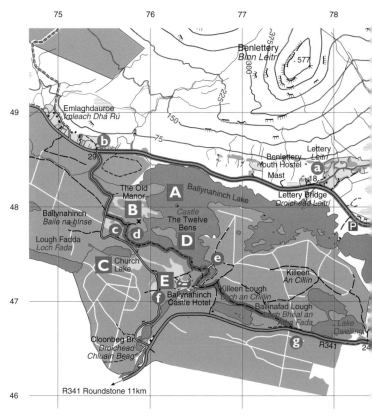

**d** The lakeshore path crosses a stone bridge over an inflowing river, then takes an undulating course through the woods. There is a view back across the lake to the Old Manor, and later to Castle Island, the main road and the peaks of Binn Ghleann Uisce and Binn Leitrí in the Twelve Bens. The path diverts away from the wooded shore to pass a house, then continues, keeping left to reach a footbridge over the outflowing river, the Abhainn Mhór, home to salmon, trout, otter and pine martens.

## D   The Twelve Bens

The historian Roderick O'Flaherty may have been looking across Ballynahinch Lough when he wrote of 'the twelve high mountains of Bennabeola, called by marriners the twelve stakes.' He highlighted one of them in particular, commenting that 'Bindowglass is the highest of them, and, next the lake, is two miles high.' While not being quite so high as two miles, Bindowglass has been equated with Bendouglas, which is another name for Binn Leitrí.

e   Don't cross the footbridge, but follow the path running downstream beside the river. This path passes some tall trees and reaches an iron gate in a stout wall. Go through the gate to reach the access road for the Ballynahinch Castle Hotel. A right turn leads straight up to the castle, while a left turn leads away from it.

### E   Ballynahinch Castle Hotel 763472

Ballynahinch Castle is a sham, built originally as a large, but rather plain, inn by Robert Martin in the late 1700s. The building was renovated in 1813 and used as a residence by 'Humanity' Dick Martin. Lavish parties were held there and many notable figures were entertained, including the great nationalists Theobald Wolfe Tone and Daniel O'Connell. Richard Martin died in 1834 with considerable debts after fleeing Ballynahinch for Boulogne in France. The Martin family were unable to hold Ballynahinch and it was sold to the Berridge family, who gave the building its present shape and structure. Eventually it came into the hands of 'Ranji, Prince of Cricketeers'. This was His Highness the Maharaja

Jam Sahib of Nawanger. He purchased the place in 1924, enjoying the scenery and fishing in particular. He landscaped the grounds and woodlands around Ballynahinch, threw lavishly exotic parties and died in 1933. The castle passed to Ranji's nephew, then to the McCormack family and by 1946 it was managed by the Irish Tourist Board. It has since been developed, with its tourism potential in mind, as an elegant hotel, with a high degree of public access to its grounds. The Castle holds a roost of Daubenton's Bat, and the extremely rare Whiskered Bat has also been recorded in the area.

The dark form of Cashel Hill is seen rising beyond the complex shoreline of Ballynahinch Lough.

**f** Follow the tarmac access road away from Ballynahinch Castle, crossing a bridge over the Abhainn Mhór. The road is lined by white stones and rock outcrops along the way have been planted with a fine variety of heathers. When the road bends right, exit to the left, crossing a stile beside a gate. A forest track rises gently to the right, crossing a clear-felled and replanted area, where care is needed as heavy forest trucks trundle through on occasion. Views take in a white lodge building near Ballynahinch Castle, off to the right. The track enters a tall stand of forest which is attractively flanked by a variety of deciduous trees, and there are also glimpses across the waters of Loch an Chillin. Later, the dark forest floor is mossy and a variety of fungi may be tracked by their odours. Keep to the right at a junction of tracks and leave the forest by crossing another stile beside a gate.

**g** Turn left to follow a minor road. This is flanked by forest at first, then there is a view across Loch Bhéal an Átha Fada, which has a fringe of oak, birch and alder, with views across to Gleann Chóchan. Note the course of an old railway trackbed running parallel to the road. The road later passes a restored railway building where there was once a level crossing, and a swampy cutting can be seen off to the right. The road runs through the scattered village of Béal an Átha Fada, where fuchsia lines the roadside. There is an old style telephone kiosk and a disused National School both spotted before the road runs alongside Loch na Brocaí. Invasive giant rhubarbs are muscling in beside the lake and the road, displacing grass, heather, bracken and even gorse bushes. The road passes a stout wall surrounding Lisnabrucky before reaching St. Joseph's Church.

**F   Lisnabrucky 797469**
Lisnabrucky is a fine hilltop mansion surrounded by an exotic

woodland. The house was built around 1915 by an American named Wilcocks. A stout wall and white iron gates enclose the grounds, where a bewildering array of trees and shrubs have been planted. St. Joseph's, just across the bridge from Lisnabrucky, was built around 1835 and enlarged in 1911, though it is still quite a small building. There is access to a fine, old and rugged graveyard containing several members of the Martin and Berridge families.

**h**  Follow the road onwards: there is a reedy portion of Ballynahinch Lough to the left and a rugged, rocky bogland to the right. The road has a fine view into the rugged recesses of Gleann Chóchan in the Twelve Bens and leads quickly to a junction with the main N59 road at Canal Stage. Turn left as indicated by a signpost reading 'Scenic Route via Clifden'. Cross the Canal Bridge and note that the river has been partially canalised. Look out for salmon, trout and otter.

### G  Canal Stage 803475

Canal Stage obtains its name partly from the canalisation of the river and partly from the fact that it was a stage on the Bianconi coach transport service early in the 19th Century. The name is still in use by both the Connemara Bus and Bus Éireann drivers. The bridge divides the Upper Ballynahinch Fishery from the Lough Inagh Fishery, for fishing permit purposes.

**i**  This walk could be completed by catching a bus back to Benlettery Youth Hostel, but the road walk is no great hardship. There is a level stretch followed by a gentle ascent to a huddle of houses at a road junction. The main road runs gently downhill to cross a bridge, where a former old bridge lies just upstream. Benlettery Youth Hostel is just to the right across the bridge.

A small group of walkers on the slopes of Binn Leitrí look across the waters of Ballynahinch Lough.

# BINN GHLEANN UISCE

**START/FINISH:**
On the main N59 road at its junction with the Barr na nÓrán road, signposted Sli Connemara, close to Our Lady of the Wayside Church. There is a small space to park just at the junction.

**DISTANCE:** 7 miles (11km).

**APPROXIMATE TIME:**
4 hours.

**HIGHEST POINT:**
1710ft (516m) Binn Ghleann Uisce.

**MAPS:** Harveys Superwalker Connemara; OS Sheets 37 & 44.

**REFRESHMENTS:**
The nearest place offering food and drink is the Connemara Heritage & History Centre, which has a restaurant, along the main road in the direction of Clifden. The only other place nearby is Ballynahinch Castle Hotel.

**ADVICE:**
This is a fairly straightforward mountain walk with direction determined by following streams on the mountainsides, but care is needed when crossing the gap or visiting the summit in mist.

**W**alkers who feel intimidated by the tougher horseshoe walks in the Twelve Bens might consider a relatively simple ascent of Binn Ghleann Uisce. The key to the ascent and descent lie not in following rugged ridges, but in following splashing streams on the flanks of the mountain. However, remember that there are no distinctly trodden paths. Views from the summit take in portions of the Twelve Bens, as well as the strange and complex watery landscape of Roundstone Bog.

**A   Our Lady of the Wayside Church 753487**
This tiny church stands just off the main N59 road close to where this walk starts. It was built as a Protestant church in 1865, but it closed in 1958. It reopened as a Catholic church in 1959 and

A Connemara Pony grazes a pasture, with the dome of Binn Ghleann Uisce in the distance.

is currently used for Mass only on Saturday evenings.

**a** There is a small amount of roadside parking where the Barr na nÓrán road joins the main N59 road. Start by walking up the Barr na nÓrán road, but only until a few fenced enclosures have been passed. Head off to the right, climbing gradually uphill on a rugged slope away from the road. Purple Moor Grass stands in tussocks, along with bog myrtle among low outcrops of rock. The aim is not to climb high straight away, but to cut across a broad and boggy slope to reach the river draining Gleann Uisce, between Binn Ghleann Uisce and Binn Leitrí.

**b** Don't cross the river in Gleann Uisce, but turn left to follow it upstream. There is only the vaguest trace of a path, though an obvious embankment has been constructed parallel to the river. A small gorge contains a handful of small oak trees which would have been quite widespread in the distant past. Note the fine little waterfall which drops in two distinct stages into the gorge.

**c** Continue upstream alongside the watercourse. Small growths of willow might be noticed as well as a frog or two, and heather begins to dominate as height is gained. Eventually, the course of the stream is lost in the heather as the ground steepens. Skirt around a bright green bog hole up to a broad gap of blanket bog and outcrops of rock is reached.

A stump of bog pine is seen in front of more recent forestry on the lower slopes of Binn Ghleann Uisce.

**d** To include the summit of Binn Ghleann Uisce, turn left on the gap. There is no real path on the broad, hummocky, bare or broken crest of rock. A prominent band of white quartz is encountered immediately before the summit cairn. There are a handful of small cairns on the summit and a whole rash of them are seen when looking towards Clifden.

**B   Binn Ghleann Uisce 766501**
Anglicised as Benglenisky, Binn Ghleann Uisce is the Peak of the Water Valley. It is only summit on this walk and rises to 1710ft (516m). Views extend all the way around the head of the

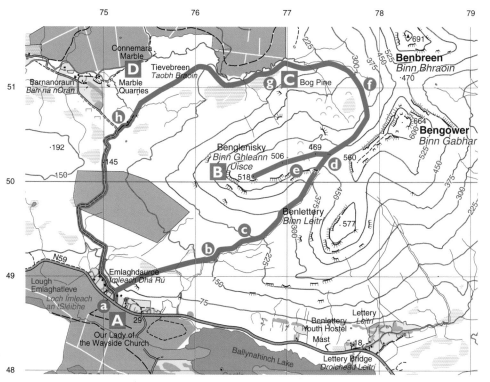

Owenglin River, taking in a good half of the Twelve Bens, including Binn Bhán, the highest one. Looking southwards the amazingly intricate little lough systems of Roundstone Bog can be studied.

**e**　Retracing steps from the summit to the broad gap, look over the edge to spot a small, heathery, grassy hump deep in the glacial coum. Take care on the descent from the gap. The ideal direction is north-east, cutting across slopes of short grass and heather. Watch for slippery patches and stony areas. Aim to cross the little gap behind the hump and walk more directly downhill, following a tongue of rugged ground between two streams.

**f**　While passing an isolated rock outcrop, note that a colony of St. Patrick's cabbage thrives out of range of grazing sheep, while foxgloves appear further downhill, beside the stream. The slope eventually levels out when the stream runs alongside a forest planted across the floor of the glen. Turn left to follow the water downstream. The easiest and driest walking is immediately beside the stream on short grass. Note the stumps of ancient pines exposed where the river has undercut the blanket bog.

## C  Bog Pine 767513

Prominent stumps of bog pine have been exposed by erosion beside the river. Following a climatic change in the Bronze Age, conditions favoured the growth of blanket bog. Another shift in the climate appears to have dried the bog sufficiently for it to be invaded by Scots Pine. However, with wetter conditions again becoming established, the inexorable growth of the bog killed the trees. The boles will have rotted and been toppled, but the roots have been very well preserved in the bog. While bog pine has sometimes been harvested and dried for fuel, these days it is simply discarded. Some imaginative artists have dried and carved the wood into exquisite ornaments.

A band of white quartz crosses the summit of Binn Ghleann Uisce, with views of the Twelve Bens beyond.

**g** Follow the river downstream until there is a prominent bend and a sudden drop into a gorge. The water exploits a band of Connemara Marble and scours out deep pools. Walk parallel to the stream, but stay well above the gorge, crossing a gentle, broad, boggy moorland slope. Eventually, begin to drift to the left to reach a small marble quarry, which is an obvious scar on the hillside. A track leads away from the quarry to join the Barr na nÓrán road.

**D   Connemara Marble 753507**

The green-banded ornamental Connemara Marble at Barr na nÓrán has been quarried since the 1820s. The first quarry was started by Thomas Martin of Ballynahinch Castle. The marble appears as a variable band in folded strata, proving difficult to locate and exploit at times.

**h** Turn left to follow the minor road gently uphill. Binn Ghleann Uisce raises its steep and rugged flanks to the left, looking quite difficult from this vantage point. The road enters a forest and descends gently, crosses another slope of bog and finally returns to the junction with the main N59 road.

A view of Binn Ghleann Uisce from the rugged gap between Binn Leitrí and Binn Gabhar.

# OWENGLIN HORSESHOE

A walk around the glacial valley of the Owenglin Horseshoe is quite rough and tough in places, with some very steep rocky or grassy ascents and descents. The pathless parts need care in mist and the whole circuit may take longer than anticipated to cover. There is an obvious escape from the deep-cut gap of Mám Eidhneach if it becomes apparent that the full round is not going to be completed. The route includes the summit of Binn Bhán, which is the highest point in Connemara and a notable viewpoint. The steep and grassy slopes of Meacanach are notable for their range of rare Alpine plants.

**A  Barr na nÓrán 744513**
Barnanoraun is the Anglicised version of Barr na nÓrán, or the Top of the Spring Wells. The scattered farmsteads are next to extensive forests and are surrounded by high mountains. Marble has been quarried here since the 1820s, when the workings were opened by Thomas Martin of Ballynahich Castle.

**a**  Cars can be driven along a narrow tarmac road and parked on a broad gravel space where a concrete bridge spans the Owenglin River. Walk back along the road, climbing past a couple of farmhouses. The road runs unfenced up a rugged, boggy slope, with fine views around the peaks of the Owenglin Horseshoe. At the top of the road a forest has been planted across a boggy gap.

**b**  Cross a muddy ditch to the left of the road and follow the forest fence up a gentle, boggy, grassy slope. Bog myrtle, bog

## START/FINISH:
At a concrete bridge spanning the Owenglin River at Barr na nÓrán.

## DISTANCE: 11 miles (18km).

## APPROXIMATE TIME:
7 hours.

## HIGHEST POINT:
2395ft (729m) on the summit of Binn Bhán, the highest point in both Connemara and County Galway.

## MAPS: Harveys Superwalker Connemara; OS Sheet 37.

## REFRESHMENTS:
The nearest place offering food and drink is the Connemara Heritage & History Centre, which has a restaurant, along the main road in the direction of Clifden. The only other place nearby is Ballynahinch Castle Hotel.

## ADVICE:
The walk around the Owenglin Horseshoe can be quite rough and rocky in places. There are some very steep slopes of rock and grass which need care, especially when wet.

Starting at Barr na nÓrán, there is a view of the deep gap between Binn Gabhar and Binn Bhraoin.

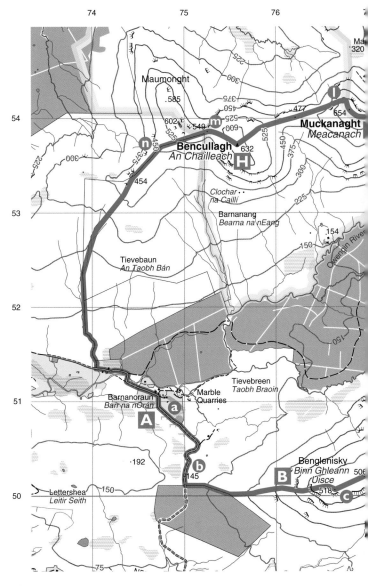

asphodel can be seen. Climbing above the forest, the slopes of Binn Ghleann Uisce become steep, rough and rocky. Pick a way up slopes of grass and heather, avoiding rock outcrops. The climbing is relentless, though the gradient eases towards the top of the mountain. A rash of little cairns are passed on a rocky shoulder just before the summit is reached.

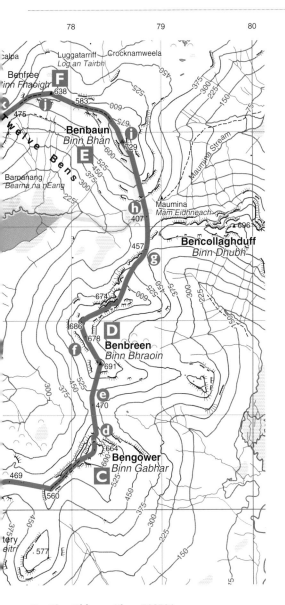

**B   Binn Ghleann Uisce 766501**

Anglicised as Benglenisky, Binn Ghleann Uisce rises to 1710ft (516m). Views extend all the way around the head of the Owenglin River, taking in a good half of the Twelve Bens, including the highest, which is Binn Bhán. Looking southwards the amazingly intricate lough systems of Roundstone Bog can be studied.

c   Leave the top of Binn Ghleann Uisce and follow the broad, rocky, hummocky crest to a broad, boggy gap. Keep walking onwards, climbing up a short, steep slope of grass, heather and scree, to reach a cairn on a hump on the ridge. Turn left and walk across a little gap. The ground then rises more steeply and the gravelly path picks its way up a blocky, rocky slope to reach the summit cairn on Binn Gabhar.

### C   Binn Gabhar 783507

Binn Gabhar, Anglicised as Bengower, is the Peak of the Goat. It is an outstanding, steep-sided mountain easily spotted in many views. Its rocky slopes rise to 2184ft (664m).

A cairn sits on a rugged hump before the steep, rocky, blocky ascent of Binn Gabhar.

d   Leaving the summit of Binn Gabhar, look down towards the next gap and locate a cairn on the slope. From this point, look for traces of a trodden path leading downhill and follow it carefully. There are five rocky places on the descent where hands will need to be used, though there are plenty of good holds. Always look downhill for evidence of a trodden path before making a move. Taken slowly and steadily, there should be no problems getting down to the gap between Binn Gabhar and Binn Bhraoin. With attention focussed closely on blocky outcrops, damp gullies, nooks and crannies, look out for small colonies of bilberry, crowberry, thrift, St. Patrick's cabbage and prostrate juniper – all occupying safe havens away from grazing sheep.

e   Binn Bhraoin rises straight up from the gap, with a steep slope of scree. Most walkers stay on a fine, worn tongue of scree, but there is better purchase for feet on the more stable, bouldery scree to the left. Even so, the ascent is a punishing treadmill of around 750ft (230m) before the summit cairn on Binn Bhraoin is finally reached.

### D  Binn Bhraoin 783516

Binn Bhraoin, Anglicised as Benbreen, appears to be named after someone called Braoin, but folklore records nothing about who he might have been. Its height is 2276ft (691m).

**f**  Continuing along the broken, rocky ridge, there are a handful of cairned summits to pass. Some walkers climb all of them, while others skirt round them on the Gleann Chóchan flank. When navigating in mist, note that the ridge is curved, and that there is another change of direction required to reach a gap at the head of Gleann Chóchan. There is a vague, trodden path down ribs and slabs of rock, ending with a grassy slope peppered with rocks on the final run down to the gap.

**g**  Drop to the left of the gap and cut diagonally northwards across the slope to reach the lower gap called Mám Eidhneach. This is the lowest of all the gaps in the Twelve Bens, at 1345ft (410m).

**h**  Binn Bhán towers above Mám Eidhneach and promises a steep and arduous ascent of 1050ft (315m). There is a grassy slope which can be followed. It is unremitting in its steepness and will seldom be climbed without a pause for breath. Avoid steep rock or scree as much as possible. Towards the top, the ground becomes quite rocky, but the gradient eases too. The summit of Binn Bhán is crowned by a concrete trig point, set within what is probably a prehistoric cairn, which is an unusual feature in Connemara.

### E  Binn Bhán 785539

Binn Bhán, Anglicised as Benbaun, is the White Peak, no doubt so named because of its bright flanks of quartzite. The summit trig point stands at an altitude of 2395ft (729m), making this the highest point in Connemara and County Galway. As a viewpoint it is excellent. Look around to spot the lake-strewn Roundstone

Descending the grassy slopes of Meacanach, there is a view back to Binn Gabhar and Binn Leitrí.

Bog, Cregg Hill and its TV masts, followed by An Chailleach, Meacanach, Binn Fhraoigh and Diamond Hill. Tully Mountain is closer to the sea, then Cnoc Breac, Binn Bhreac and Maolan give way to Dúchruach and Maolchnoc. Across Killary Harbour rise Mweelrea, Sheeffry Hills and Binn Gorm. Leenane Hill and the Devilsmother can be seen, as well as Binn Bhriocáin, Cnoc na hUillean and Binn Idir an Dá Log in the Maum Turk Mountains. Binn an Choire Bhig, Binn Chorr, Binn Dhubh, Binn Dhoire Chláir, Binn Bhraoin and Binn Ghleann Uisce complete the view of the Twelve Bens which are closer to hand.

i  Follow the broad, rocky, stony crest of Binn Bhán down to the next gap. There is a vaguely trodden path which passes a few grassy patches, but is mostly on rock, where almost every footfall makes a crunching sound. There are little tufts of grass, otherwise nothing breaks the uncompromisingly stony surface apart from a few clubmosses, tiny cushions of thrift and small rosettes of St. Patrick's cabbage. After leaving the stony slope and crossing the boggy gap, there is a short, steep, smooth grassy ascent to the top of Binn Fhraoigh.

**F  Binn Fhraoigh 777544**
Binn Fhraiogh is Anglicised as Benfree and means Heather Mountain. This seems strange for a summit of close-cropped grass, but things change in time, including vegetation cover. The cairn stands at 2095ft (638m).

j  Leaving the top of Binn Fhraoigh, a steep slope of grass, peppered with stones, leads downhill. There is a slight break of slope, then the descent continues straight down to a low-slung gap where there are a couple of boggy humps to cross around 1540ft (470m).

k  Rising above the gap is another very steep, grassy slope. This rises to a rocky prow which needs to be side-stepped. There is a chance to pause for breath on a level stance, otherwise the climb is unremitting and few walkers will reach the top without puffing and blowing! The upper slope bears a scattering of stones, then there is a grassy crest with a cairn. The true summit of Meacanach, however, lies a little further along the grassy crest, marked by another cairn.

**G  Meacanach 767541**
Anglicised as Muckanaght, Meacanach translates as Pig-like, possibly from its boar-head profile in some views. Composed of schist, rather than quartzite, the mountain is less rocky than the rest of the Twelve Bens, but its grassy slopes are remarkably

steep and slippery. Extreme caution is needed in wet and windy weather. The summit cairn stands at 2153ft (654m). Meacanach is notable for its range of rare Alpine plants. These include mountain sorrel, mountain willow, Alpine saw-wort, Alpine meadow-rue and purple saxifrage.

**I** Descend from Meacanach on a slope of grass and moss to reach a gap covered by blanket bog. Climb uphill on short grass, heather and moss, which is peppered with stones, swinging left near the top to reach the summit cairn. There is an outcrop of white quartz near the summit of An Chailleach.

### H An Chailleach 755537
An Chailleach is Anglicised as Bencullagh and means The Old Woman. The summit cairn stands at 2084ft (632m).

**m** Leaving the top of An Chailleach, walk down a heather slope, which becomes rockier towards the next gap. A switchback ridge bears another cairn: turn left after the cairn and follow a steep, crunchy scree path downhill. The slope continues as steep, short heather, becoming grassier towards the next gap. Cross the gap, where there is decaying blanket bog, and make a short ascent to a little summit of grass and heather, with a craggy face to the right. This is the last little summit on the Owenglin Horseshoe.

**n** Turn left on the summit to follow a rounded crest of decaying blanket bog towards the Owenglin River and Barr na nÓrán. Drift to the right before reaching a boggier part of the crest. Drop down into a small valley of grass, heather and rushes. Look across a slope of tussocky grass to spot the corner of a fence. Simply follow the fence and an accompanying bouldery stream downhill. When a track is reached at the foot of the slope, turn left to pass a white cottage and farm buildings to return to the concrete bridge over the Owenglin River where the walk started.

A farm access road is reached near a white farmhouse at the completion of the Owenglin Horseshoe.

# GLEANN MHÓR HORSESHOE

**START/FINISH:**
On the main N59 where a track leads from a road bend to a restored limekiln. Parking is not possible at this point, so motorists may need to start from the car park at the nearby Kylemore Abbey.

**DISTANCE:** 10 miles (16km).

**APPROXIMATE TIME:**
6 hours.

**HIGHEST POINT:**
2153ft (654m) on the summit of Meacanach.

**MAPS:** Harveys Superwalker Connemara; OS Sheet 37.

**REFRESHMENTS:**
None actually on the route. The nearest place offering food is the restaurant at Kylemore Abbey.

**ADVICE:**
The walk around the Gleann Mhór Horseshoe is quite rugged. There are some steep climbs, especially onto Meacanach, which could be tricky in wet weather.

**T**he Connemara National Park is based on Gleann Mhór on the flanks of the Twelve Bens. A walk around the glacial valley of the Gleann Mhór Horseshoe takes in all the mountains contained in the National Park, proving to be a strenuous undertaking. The 'nails' in the horseshoe include Cnoc Breac, Binn Bhreac, the steep-sided Meacanach and rugged An Chailleach. A walk along the broad, boggy, grassy floor of Gleann Mhór is followed by a route across the flanks of Cnoc Breac and a retracing of steps to the main road. If Meacanach proves too steep to climb, then there is an escape from the previous gap down into Gleann Mhór.

**a** There is nowhere to park cars beside the main N59 where the access track runs towards a restored limekiln. Cars could be parked at nearby Kylemore Abbey, then the main N59 road could be followed to reach the track. At the start of the walk there is a gate flanked by stout iron gateposts, recessed from a bend in the road at 752581, and a prominent sign for the Connemara National Park is located at the junction of the main road and the track. The track passes through an area planted with alder.

### A   Limekiln 755577
A large, restored limekiln stands at the end of the access track, beside a long slit of a quarry at the foot of Maolan. Water from a nearby Holy Well has long been tapped to supply Kylemore Abbey.

**b** Have a look at the limekiln, then follow the track away to the right. The track leads to a gateway in a deer fence. Don't go through the gate, but stay on the track and cross a river, continuing across a broad, grassy bog. The surface is often stony and there is a water-filled drainage ditch alongside. Gorse, rhododendron, holly, ash, foxglove, St. Dabeoc's heath and purple

A view of Diamond Hill, Tully Mountain and the coast from the top of Cnoc Breac after a steep climb.

A view towards Diamond Hill, with the Polladirk River alongside, seen from the steep slopes of Meacanach.

moor grass line the track. It crosses the ditch, where a bridge is planned, and continues through rhododendron scrub to pass close to Kylemore Farm.

### B   Kylemore Farm 744579
Kylemore Farm is part of the Kylemore Abbey complex. The Benedictine nuns practise traditional farming methods. There is no public access to the farm or the land immediately around it, or directly to or from Kylemore Abbey.

c   The track bears left, then crosses   a boggy area with clumps of rhododendron and gorse scrub. There is a metal step stile over a deer fence, and a muddy path runs upstream alongside the Polladirk River into more patches of rhododendron scrub. There is a footbridge over the river, but don't cross it. Instead, continue upstream and cross another little metal foootbridge to the left of the river.

d   Climb uphill on a slope of tussocky grass. There is a level stance, then the slope becomes steep and pathless all the way to the summit of Cnoc Breac. The grassy slope runs up to rocky outcrops, which can be outflanked, then there is more heather than grass and many embedded boulders litter the steep upper slopes. The gradient eases towards the top, then the crest of the hill has low rock outcrops and a cairn on the summit. Wildlife and flora to look for: oxes, ravens and Irish hares, juniper, crowberry and bearberry.

### C   Cnoc Breac 749566
Cnoc Breac is Anglicised as Knockbrack, meaning Speckled Hill. The summit rises to 1460ft (442m).

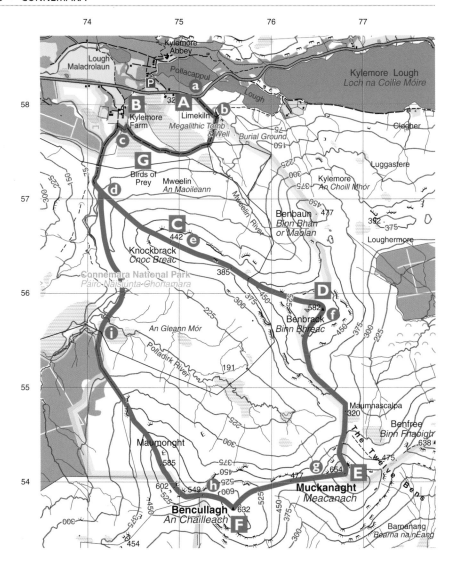

e  Walk along a broad, heathery, mossy, stony crest to drop down to a gap, then climb up to a deer fence. Climb the deer fence in a manner prescribed by Connemara National Park staff, where the ratchets on the straining posts give a good purchase for feet. Ladder stiles may eventually be installed at popular crossing points. Continue straight uphill and keep to the left of a rock outcrop, then keep left of a highly contorted outcrop (spot the St. Patrick's cabbage). Keep climbing up the rugged slopes to reach the hummocky top of Binn Bhreac.

There are a handful of summits bearing cairns.

### D   Binn Bhreac 766558
Binn Bhreac is Anglicised as Benbrack, meaning the Speckled Peak. Its summit rises to a height of 1922ft (582m).

**f**   Pick a way down a series of little rocksteps to reach the next gap, but pause on the way to study the exceptionally steep northern face of Meacanach, which is to be climbed next on the circuit. (Faint-hearted walkers can exit to the right, rather than climb Meacanach, and carefully pick a way down into the boggy recesses of Gleann Mhór.) Cross a gap and start climbing up a steep, grassy slope. This slope gets steeper, becoming mossy and slippery in places. The slabs of rock are a treacherously greasy schist, which should be avoided. Pick a route with care, always keeping feet firmly planted and zig-zag to avoid rock outcrops at a higher level. When the gradient begins to ease, the summit cairn will be seen.

### E   Meacanach 767541
Anglicised as Muckanaght, Meacanach translates as Pig-like, probably from its boar-like profile in some views. There are views of Tully Mountain, Diamond Hill, Maolchnoc, Mweelrea, Sheeffry Hills, Binn Gorm, Leenane Hill, Devilsmother, Maum Turk Mountains, Binn Bhán, Binn Braoin, Binn Gabhar, Binn Ghleann Uisce, Errisbeg, An Chailleach and stretches of the coastline beyond. The mountain is composed of schist, rather than quartzite, and so is less rocky than the rest of the Twelve Bens, but its grassy slopes are remarkably steep. The summit cairn stands at 2153ft (654m). Meacanach is notable for its range of rare Alpine plants. These include mountain sorrel, mountain willow, Alpine saw-wort, Alpine meadow-rue and purple saxifrage.

**g**   Descend from Meacanach on a slope of grass and moss to reach a gap covered by blanket bog. Climb uphill on short grass, heather and moss, which is peppered with stones, swinging left near the top to reach the summit cairn. There is an outcrop of white quartz near the summit of An Chailleach.

### F   An Chailleach 755537
The last summit on the Gleann Mhór Horseshoe is An Chailleach, Anglicised as Bencullagh, and means the Old Woman. The summit cairn stands at 2084ft (632m).

**h**   Leaving the top of An Chailleach, walk down a heather slope, which becomes rockier towards the next gap. A switchback ridge bears a couple of cairns, then there is a steep descent. A slope of

Looking back around the Gleann Mhór Horseshoe from the foot of An Chailleach, Meacanach is prominent.

heather, grass and broken rock leads down to the deer fence on the lower slopes. Cross the fence, then turn left to follow it across the boggy floor of Gleann Mhór. There are some vague paths across the bog,

i  The Polladirk River drains Gleann Mhór, running through a deep gorge between Cnoc Breac and Diamond Hill. It is possible to cross the river at a shallow point before the deep gorge and pick a way across the slopes of Cnoc Breac, high above the river, using a sort of rugged terrace across the flank of the mountain. Looking ahead, drift down gradually towards a footbridge spanning the river, but don't cross it. All that remains is to retrace the earlier steps of the day, following the track across the lower slopes of Cnoc Breac, from Kylemore Farm to the restored limekiln and so out onto the main road. If a car is parked at Kylemore Abbey, then turn left to reach it.

In the foreground is the moorland slope which is followed above the Polladirk River gorge towards the end of the walk.

## G  Birds of Prey

The area around Kylemore and Maolan offers perhaps the best opportunity to see the full range of birds of prey in Connemara. The little merlin is fairly common, hunting between the coast and lower areas of bog. The kestrel is more easily identified because of its singular hunting method, hovering mostly over open ground, though it will sometimes perch on a tree to scan an area. The sparrowhawk prefers wooded areas, and more particularly deciduous woods, so Kylemore is one of its haunts. The peregrine is the largest bird of prey in Ireland and it will hunt over both the glens and the higher mountains. It is most likely to be spotted after uttering a piercing scream in flight. The mountains remain largely the preserve of the raven, which will readily mob even the peregrine for approaching its terrain.

# CNOC BREAC, BINN BHREAC AND MAOLAN

The Maolan Horseshoe offers a fine short walk giving a sample of walking in the Twelve Bens. There are three summits in the circuit; Cnoc Breac, Binn Bhreac and Maolan. In clear weather, there are superb views over Kylemore Abbey, Kylemore Lough and Kylemore Pass. The walk is just inside the confines of the Connemara National Park, and while it has a good access track, there is no parking nearer than Kylemore Abbey. The circuit includes very steep ascent and descent routes.

**a** There is nowhere to park cars beside the main N59 where the access track runs towards a restored limekiln. Cars could be parked at nearby Kylemore Abbey, then the main N59 road could be followed to reach the track. There is nothing to mark the start except a gateway flanked by stout iron gateposts, recessed from a bend in the road at 752581. The track passes through an area planted with alder.

### A Limekiln 755577
A large, restored limekiln stands at the end of the access track, beside a long slit of a quarry at the foot of Maolan. Water from a nearby Holy Well has long been tapped to supply Kylemore Abbey.

**b** Have a look at the limekiln, then follow the track away to the right. The track leads to a gateway in a deer fence. Don't

**START/FINISH:**
On the main N59 where a track leads from a road bend to a restored limekiln. Parking is not possible at this point, so motorists may need to start from the car park at the nearby Kylemore Abbey.

**DISTANCE:** 6 miles (9.5km).

**APPROXIMATE TIME:**
4 hours.

**HIGHEST POINT:**
1922ft (582m) on the summit of Binn Bhreac.

**MAPS:** Harveys Superwalker Connemara; OS Sheet 37.

**REFRESHMENTS:**
None actually on the route. The nearest place offering food is the restaurant at Kylemore Abbey.

**ADVICE:**
This is a fairly short walk, but the ascent and descent routes are very steep and need to be taken carefully when wet.

The steep, rugged, pathless slopes of Cnoc Breac are climbed at the start of the day's walk.

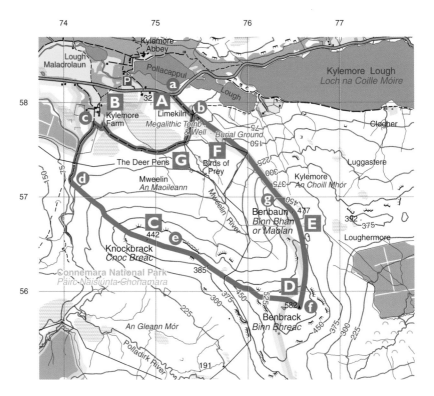

go through the gate, but stay on the track and cross a river, continuing across a broad, grassy bog. The surface is often stony and there is a water-filled drainage ditch alongside, where you are likely to see gorse, rhododendron, holly, ash, foxglove, St. Dabeoc's heath and purple moor grass. The track crosses the ditch, where a bridge is planned to be built, and continues through rhododendron scrub to pass close to Kylemore Farm.

### B Kylemore Farm 744579
Kylemore Farm is part of the Kylemore Abbey complex. The Benedictine nuns practise traditional farming methods on the land. There is no public access to the farm or the land immediately around it, or directly to or from Kylemore Abbey.

c The track bears left, crossing a boggy area with clumps of rhododendron and gorse scrub. There is a metal step stile over a deer fence, and a muddy path runs upstream alongside the Polladirk River into more patches of rhododendron scrub. There is a footbridge over the river, but don't cross it. Instead, continue upstream and cross another little metal foootbridge to the left of the river.

**d** Climb uphill on a slope of tussocky grass. There is a level stance, then the slope becomes steep and pathless all the way to the summit of Cnoc Breac. The grassy slope runs up to rocky outcrops, which can be outflanked, then there is more heather than grass and many embedded boulders litter the steep upper slopes. The gradient eases towards the top, then the crest of the hill has low rock outcrops and a cairn on the

Looking to Cnoc Breac, Diamond Hill and Tully Mountain from the slopes of Binn Bhreac.

summit. During the climb, you might come across foxes, ravens and Irish hares.

**C Cnoc Breac 749566**
Cnoc Breac is Anglicised as Knockbrack, meaning Speckled Hill. The summit rises to 1460ft (442m).

**e** Walk along a broad, heathery, mossy, stony crest to drop down to a gap, then climb up to a deer fence. Climb the deer fence in a manner prescribed by Connemara National Park staff, where the ratchets on the straining posts give a good purchase for feet. Ladder stiles may eventually be installed at popular crossing points. Continue straight uphill and keep to the left of a rock outcrop, then keep left of a highly contorted outcrop. Keep climbing up the rugged slopes to reach the hummocky top of Binn Bhreac. There are a handful of summits bearing cairns.

An almost aerial view over Kylemore Lough from the steep, grassy slopes of Maolan at the start of the descent.

### D  Binn Bhreac 766558

Binn Bhreac is Anglicised as Benbrack, meaning the Speckled Peak. It summit rises to a height of 1922ft (582m). Views extend to Achill Island, Dúchruach, Maolchnoc, Mweelree, Sheefry Hills, Binn Gorm, Leenane Hill, Maumtrasna, Maum Turk Mountains, Binn Bhán, Binn Bhraoin, Binn Gabhar, Meacanach, An Chailleach, Cregg Hill and a good stretch of coastline round to Diamond Hill.

f  Leaving the summit by turning left, there is a vague, stony path running down a steep and rocky ridge towards Maolan. The ridge becomes more gently graded, then drops again to a boggy gap crossed by a fence. The fence can be followed straight up a short, steep, grassy slope onto Maolan. There is a small cairn just to the right of the fence.

### E  Maolan 765568

The Ordnance Survey label this point as Benbaun, but it is Maolan, meaning the Little Bald Hill. The little summit cairn stands at 1577ft (477m) and there are especially fine views over Kylemore Abbey, Kylemore Lough and the Kylemore Pass, with Dúchruach rising opposite.

g  Descend from Maolan by following the crest of the hill towards Kylemore Abbey. The ground steepens greatly and there are rocky ribs. Keep to the right of any rock, walking down a steep slope of grass and moss. If views are to be enjoyed, then stand still, as a slip due to a loss of concentration could have unhappy consequences. The aim is to reach a knobbly little ridge far below, which bears short grass and clumps of rushes – look out for whinchats. A couple of gnarled hawthorns are passed on the lower slopes, and a long slit of an old quarry leads to the limekiln which was inspected earlier in the day. All that remains is to retrace the earlier steps of the day, following the track across the lower slopes of Cnoc Breac, from Kylemore Farm to the restored limekiln and so out onto the main road. If a car is parked at Kylemore Abbey, then turn left to reach it.

## F Birds of Prey

The area around Kylemore and Maolan offers perhaps the best opportunity to see the full range of birds of prey in Connemara. The little merlin is fairly common, hunting between the coast and lower areas of bog. The kestrel is more easily identified because of its singular hunting method, hovering mostly over open ground, though it will sometimes perch on a tree to scan an area. The sparrowhawk prefers wooded areas, and more particularly deciduous woods, so Kylemore is one of its haunts. The peregrine is the largest bird of prey in Ireland and it will hunt over both the glens and the higher mountains. It is most likely to be spotted after uttering a piercing scream in flight. The mountains remain largely the preserve of the raven, which will readily mob even the peregrine for approaching its terrain.

## G The Deer Pens

Situated at the foot of Maolan, the deer pens are used to raise red deer for release into the Connemara National Park. The animals are native to Ireland, having been brought in from stock in the Killarney National Park. A deer fence has been erected which encloses Gleann Mhór and Diamond Hill. This marks the full extent of the red deer's range. Deer have been missing from the Connemara landscape for some time, though the historian Roderick O'Flaherty commented that 'in the confines of Balynahynsy, Ross, and Moycullin countreys … the fat deere is frequently hunted.'

A wind-blasted hawthorn at the foot of Maolan towards the end of the short horseshoe walk.

# GLEANN CARBAD HORSESHOE

**START/FINISH:**
At the junction of the R344 road and the farm access road leading into Gleann Carbad. Parking at the mouth of Gleann Carbad is very limited. Either park very considerately off the access road, perhaps beside the bridge, or ask permission to park.

**DISTANCE:** 10 miles (16km).

**APPROXIMATE TIME:** 6 hours.

**HIGHEST POINT:** 2395ft (729m) on the summit of Binn Bhán, the highest point in Connemara and County Galway.

**MAPS:** Harveys Superwalker Connemara; OS Sheet 37.

**REFRESHMENTS:** None on the route. The Pass Inn Hotel is easily reached at the junction of the R344 and the main N59 road. The Lough Inagh Lodge is further away in the other direction.

**ADVICE:** The Gleann Carbad Horseshoe is a mountain walk with some very steep slopes and plenty of rock and bog. The ascent and descent of Meacanach is on very steep grass.

Gleann Carbad is one of a handful of glacial valleys cut into the rocky flanks of the Twelve Bens. A walk around it takes in several summits, including Binn Bhán, which is the highest mountain in Connemara. The steep-sided grassy mountain of Meacanach needs special care, but in case of difficulty there is an early descent into Gleann Carbad available from a preceeding gap. There are some particularly long and steep ascents and descents to be endured while completing the Gleann Carbad Horseshoe.

**A   Gleann Carbad 795574**
Anglicised as Glencorbet, the name of Gleann Carbad has been translated as both the Valley of Chariots and the Valley of Boulders. The latter seems more appropriate. The little farmsteads are exploiting a small area of fertile limestone in the glen, with rough grazing available on the mountainsides. Remember that parking is very limited at the start of this walk.

**a**   The narrow tarmac access road leaves the R344 road near Kylemore and crosses a bridge over the Kylemore River. The bridge is founded on a limestone outcrop. There are only a handful of buildings, and when the tarmac comes to an end there is a stony track heading off to the left.

**b**   Follow the track, but leave it early to start climbing uphill. The slope is fairly gentle, and there are tilted blocks of quartzite with stones lying scattered on the grassy patches. At a higher level the ground is wetter, but still scattered with stones. There is a little limestone hill which is distinguished by having short, green grass in contrast to the browner, longer moor grass elsewhere.

**c**   Cross a junction of fences in a dip and continue up a rougher, boggier crest of grass and heather. The crest is quite hummocky, but the general trend is uphill. There is a short, steep, rocky slope down to a boggy gap, then a steep, grassy ascent onto Maolan.

**B   Maolan 765568**
Maolan is the Little Bald Hill, although the Ordnance Survey record it as Benbaun, or Binn Bhán, meaning the White Mountain. There is a small cairn on top at an altitude of 1577ft (477m). Views over Kylemore Abbey, Kylemore Pass and Kylemore Lough are particularly good, as there is an immense sense of space.

**d** There is the end of a fence near the summit cairn on Maolan: go round it, then follow it down a short, steep slope to cross a boggy gap. Climb uphill, keeping right of the fence to reach a rough and rocky ridge. The ridge is easier to walk than it looks, bearing a gravelly path and rock outcrops which are almost like stairways. Simply climb over the rock, or along strips of heather, to reach the top of Binn Bhreac. The summit area is quite broad and hummocky, with a handful of little tops bearing cairns.

**C  Binn Bhreac 766558**
Binn Bhreac is the Speckled Mountain, Anglicised as Benbrack, rising to a height of 1922ft (582m) at the summit cairn.

The farm access road serving a handful of farmsteads in Gleann Carbad, with Maolan rising beyond.

**e** Pick a way down a series of little rocksteps to reach the next gap, but pause on the way to study the exceptionally steep northern face of Meacanach, which is to be climbed next on the circuit. (Faint-hearted walkers can exit to the left, rather than climb Meacanach, then pick a way down to the forested head of Gleann Mhór.) Cross a gap and start climbing up a steep, grassy slope. This slope gets steeper, becoming mossy and slippery in places. The slabs of rock are a treacherously greasy schist, which

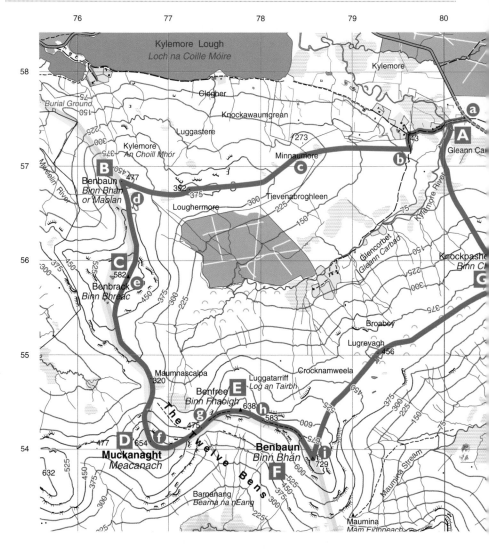

should be avoided. Pick a route with care, always keeping feet firmly planted and zig-zag to avoid rock outcrops at a higher level. When the gradient begins to ease, the summit cairn will be seen.

### D Meacanach 767541

Anglicised as Muckanaght, Meacanach translates as Pig-like, probably from its boar-like profile in some views. The mountain is composed of schist, rather than quartzite, and so is less rocky than the rest of the Twelve Bens, but its grassy slopes are

remarkably steep. The summit cairn stands at 2153ft (654m). Meacanach is notable for its range of rare Alpine plants. These include mountain sorrel, mountain willow, Alpine saw-wort, Alpine meadow-rue and purple saxifrage.

**f** Turn left to leave the cairn on top of Meacanach. There is a short walk along a gentle, grassy crest, passing another little cairn, then the ground bears a scattering of stones and begins to fall more steeply. At the top of a rocky prow there is a sudden very steep grassy slope leading down to a low-slung gap. Pick a way carefully downhill to reach the gap, where there are two boggy humps to cross at around 1540ft (470m).

**g** Another steep slope of grass leads uphill, sometimes peppered with stones. There is a slight break of slope, otherwise the ascent is unremitting and the top of Binn Fhraoigh is gained only after considerable puffing and blowing!

### E Binn Fhraoigh 777544

Binn Fhraiogh is Anglicised as Benfree and means Heather Mountain. This seems strange for a summit of close-cropped grass, but things change in time, including vegetation cover. The cairn stands at 2095ft (638m).

**h** There is a short, steep, grassy descent from Binn Fhraoigh, then the terrain changes to a broken, stony, rocky ridge leading up to Binn Bhán. There is a vaguely trodden path, which passes a few grassy patches but is mostly on rock, where almost every footfall makes a crunching sound. There are little tufts of grass, otherwise nothing breaks the uncompromisingly stony surface apart from a few clubmosses, tiny cushions of thrift and small rosettes of St. Patrick's cabbage. The summit of Binn Bhán is marked by a rare feature in Connemara – a concrete trig point.

The summit cairn on Binn Fhraoigh, looking back across a deeply-cut gap to Meacanach.

## F   Binn Bhán 785539

Binn Bhán, Anglicised as Benbaun, is the White Peak, no doubt so named because of its bright flanks of quartzite. The summit trig point stands at an altitude of 2395ft (729m), making this the highest point in Connemara and County Galway. As a viewpoint it is excellent. Look around to spot the lake-strewn Roundstone Bog, Cregg Hill and its TV masts, followed by An Chailleach, Meacanach, Binn Fhraoigh and Diamond Hill. Tully Mountain is closer to the sea, then Cnoc Breac, Binn Bhreac and Maolan give way to Dúchruach and Maolchnoc. Across Killary Harbour rise

A stony, bouldery shoulder of Binn Bhán gives way suddenly to the grassy dome of Binn Fhraoigh.

Mweelrea, Sheeffry Hills and Binn Gorm. Leenane Hill and the Devilsmother can be seen, as well as Binn Bhriocáin, Cnoc na hUillean and Binn Idir an Dá Log in the Maum Turk Mountains. Binn an Choire Bhig, Binn Chorr, Binn Dhubh, Binn Dhoire Chláir, Binn Bhraoin and Binn Ghleann Uisce complete the view of the Twelve Bens which are closer to hand.

i   Leave the top of Binn Bhán by walking roughly northwards along the stony crest. Aim to locate a stony zig-zag path which drops from one rocky slab to another. Finding the path is not essential, as the slabs are pitched at an easy angle for walking. The rocky flank leads down to a stony, hummocky area, suddenly giving way to a broad, hummocky crest of blanket bog. Keep to the broad crest where there is a vaguely trodden path and only occasional outcrops of rock. There are fine views along the Inagh Valley and towards the Maum Turk Mountains. Keep to the crest to reach the rocky prow, Binn Charrach, at the end.

### G   Binn Charrach 807557

The Ordnance Survey records this little summit as Knockpasheemore, but locally it is Binn Charrach, or the Scabby Peak. There is a cairn at 1362ft (412m).

A walker crosses the hummocky, stony slopes between Binn Bhán and Binn Charrach.

j   Retrace steps slightly from the top of Binn Charrach, then drop down into Gleann Carbad. There are rocky areas on the slope of bog and grass, while halfway down there are some steep slabs to avoid. Aim for the bridge crossing the Kylemore River near the farms. There is an expanse of sloppy bog to cross, but there is a firmer footing available beside the river. Pass an old bridge and cross some 'lazy beds', where potatoes were once grown, to reach the narrow tarmac farm road at the next bridge. Turn right to return to the R344 road by following the farm road across the bog.

# GLEANN EIDHNEACH HORSESHOE

**START/FINISH:**
At the junction of the R344 road and the narrow farm road serving Gleann Eidhneach. Note that cars are not permitted into Gleann Eidhneach and there are no parking places nearby on the R344 road. It may be an idea to arrange for a lift to the start.

**DISTANCE:** 8 miles (13km).

**APPROXIMATE TIME:**
5 hours.

**HIGHEST POINT:**
2395ft (729m) on the summit of Binn Bhán, the highest point in both Connemara and County Galway.

**MAPS:** Harveys Superwalker Connemara; OS Sheet 37.

**REFRESHMENTS:**
None actually on the route, though the Pass Inn Hotel can be found at the junction of the R344 road with the main N59 road. The Lough Inagh Lodge is in the other direction.

**ADVICE:**
As a courtesy, you should seek permission to walk in Gleann Eidhneach. Ask at the farm. The walk around the Gleann Eidhneach Horseshoe features some very steep and rocky slopes, and there are some deep-cut gaps to cross. There is an obvious escape at the low gap of Mám Eidhneach if the ascent of Binn Bhán is going to lead to a late finish.

The Gleann Eidhneach Horseshoe is a rough and rocky round in the Twelve Bens, based on a fine glacial valley. It starts with a steep and rocky ascent, then covers a handful of summits separated by quite deeply-cut gaps. There are some considerable ascents on the way to Binn Bhán. The descent via the broad and boggy ridge to Binn Charrach is of a quite different quality. The ascent of Binn an Choire Bhig is steep and unremitting, and it is better to climb onto the horseshoe this way than to try and descend from it, especially in misty or wet weather, when the slope could be treacherous.

a   Parking is not permitted on the access road serving Gleann Eidhneach, nor are there any nearby parking spaces beside the R344 road between Kylemore and Loch Inagh. It may be a good idea to arrange a lift for this walk. The access road climbs uphill and passes a house next to a few trees: holly, sycamore, alder, fuchsia. Continue through a gate and pass a few farm buildings, then turn left onto a stony track. Almost immediately, turn left again to follow a vague path down a boggy slope. Look out for a line of boulders on a heathery rise.

### A   Stone Row 815551
A row of six rounded boulders stand in a line in the middle of Gleann Eidhneach. They may date from the Bronze Age and may mark some important alignment.

*A shoulder of Binn Chorr is reached, then a deep and rocky gap is crossed before rocky Binn Dhubh is traversed.*

**b**  Leave the Stone Row and drop down to a river. This is usually easily forded in dry weather, but it can flood after heavy rain and prove impassable. It's best to discover the state of this river early in the day! After fording the river, rise gently across a bog, admire the purple moor grass, heather, bog myrtle, and start climbing more and more steeply on the slopes of Binn an Choire Bhig. Looking uphill on the pathless slope, there is a large area of bare rock, which needs to be outflanked to left or right. Climbing to the left, there are stony patches in the heather, as well as a series of little rocky outcrops to be outflanked, and care is needed choosing a route all the way to the summit. Note that it is better to be climbing this slope early in the day than to be descending it late in the day, especially in poor weather.

The concrete trig point on the summit of Binn Bhán marks the highest point in Connemara and County Galway.

**B  Binn an Choire Bhig 816533**
Anglicised as Bencorrbeg, Binn an Choire Bhig is the Mountain of the Small Corrie, referring to the corrie to the south of the summit. There is a small cairn on the summit dome of rock at an altitude of 1908ft (577m). Views take in part of the Twelve Bens, most of the Maum Turk Mountains and other features.

**c**  Looking ahead, the rounded ridge is a jumble of rock outcrops and boulders, with patches of grass and heather. There is a trodden path, which is at best intermittent, crossing two gaps separated by a rugged hump. The next ascent is steep and rocky, scattered with stones, but not too difficult. There is a cairn on top of Binn an tSaighdiúra.

**C  Binn an tSaighdiúra 812528**
Binn an tSaighdiúra is the Soldier's Peak. According to local tales, a soldier, assisting with the Ordnance Survey by taking distant sightings from the higher Binn Chorr during spells of clear weather, fell from this summit to his death. The height of the mountain is 2145ft (653m).

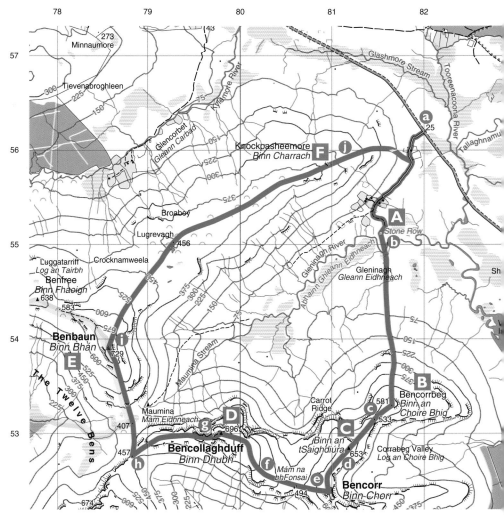

**d** The rocky ridge becomes a roller-coaster. The way ahead is stony at first, with cushions of thrift, then becomes more bouldery and features clumps of St. Patrick's cabbage. There are broad slabs streaked with quartz, then a path runs up a broken ridge to a small cairn. Continue to a larger cairn a short way down along the ridge from where there are fine views around the Gleann Chóchan Horseshoe.

**e** Turn right to walk steeply downhill on a stony path, ending on bare rock before dropping onto a strip of blanket bog hemmed in by a rock-walled notch of a gap. The gap is around 1640ft (500m).

**f** Walk uphill on an extensive slope of bare quartzite. The gradient becomes gentler, but the ground remains predominantly rocky. Ribs and slabs of rock, as well as bouldery ground, leads to the summit cairn on Binn Dhubh.

### D   Binn Dhubh 798530

Binn Dhubh, Anglicised as Bencollaghduff, is the Black Mountain, rising to 2280ft (696m). The name might have been applied by early inhabitants of Gleann Eidhneach as the steep, rocky, northern slopes seldom catch direct sunlight.

**g** Continue along the broad and bouldery summit, then take care over the descent to Mám Eidhneach. A steep, rocky drop requires the use of hands, but there are plenty of holds. The descent comes in three stages, using fairly clear gravel paths with distinct rocky shoulders in between. A descent on steep and broken rock leads down to a gap, where a sharp right turn leads across a slope to the lowest gap of Mám Eidhneach at around 1345ft (410m).

**h** Binn Bhán towers above Mám Eidhneach and promises a steep and arduous ascent. There is a grassy slope which can be followed, unremitting in its steepness and seldom climbed without a pause for breath. Towards the top, the ground becomes rocky, but the gradient eases too. The summit of Binn Bhán is crowned by a concrete trig point, which is an unusual feature in Connemara.

### E   Binn Bhán 785539

Binn Bhán, Anglicised as Benbaun, is the White Peak, no doubt so named because of its bright flanks of quartzite. The summit trig point stands at an altitude of 2395ft (729m), making this the highest point in Connemara and County Galway. As a viewpoint it is excellent. Look around to spot the lake-strewn Roundstone Bog, Cregg Hill and its TV masts, followed by An Chailleach, Meacanach, Binn Fhraoigh and Diamond Hill. Tully Mountain is closer to the sea, then Cnoc Breac, Binn Bhreac and Maolan give way to Dúchruach and Maolchnoc. Across Killary Harbour rise Mweelrea, Sheeffry Hills and Binn Gorm. Leenane Hill and the Devilsmother can be seen, as well as Binn Bhriocáin, Cnoc na hUillean and Binn Idir an Dá Log in the Maum Turk Mountains. Binn an Choire Bhig, Binn Chorr, Binn Dhubh, Binn Dhoire Chláir, Binn Bhraoin and Binn Ghleann Uisce complete the view of the Twelve Bens which are closer to hand.

**i** Leave the top of Binn Bhán by walking roughly northwards

The lower stony slopes of Binn Bhán, with a view across Gleann Eidhneach to Binn an Choire Bhig.

along the stony crest. Aim to locate a stony zig-zag path which drops from one rocky slab to another. Finding the path is not essential, as the slabs are pitched at an easy angle for walking. The rocky flank leads down to a stony, hummocky area, suddenly giving way to a broad, hummocky crest of blanket bog. Keep to the broad crest, where there is a vaguely trodden path and only occasional outcrops of rock. There are fine views along the Inagh Valley and towards the Maum Turk Mountains. Keep to the crest to reach the rocky prow at the end, which is called Binn Charrach. '

### F  Binn Charrach 807557

The Ordnance Survey records this little summit as Knockpasheemore, but it is locally called Binn Charrach, or the Scabby Peak. There is a cairn at 1362ft (412m).

**j**  Descend from Binn Charrach roughly in the direction of the road junction where the Gleann Eidhneach farm access road joins the R344 road. Don't drift too far to the left where there is more rugged ground, nor too far to the right where there are awkward areas of bracken. However, on the lower part of the broad ridge, swing to the right to reach an unfenced stretch of the farm access road. When the road is reached, turn left to return to the R344 road.

The cairn at the end of the ridge on Binn Charrach, with a view across to the Maum Turk Mountains.

# BINN CHORR HORSESHOE

One of the most rugged and rocky walks in the Twelve Bens approaches Binn Chorr from Lough Inagh. A fine circuit can be arranged linking Binn an Choire Bhig, Binn Chorr and Binn Dhoire Chláir, tracking round the heads of awesome glacial coums. The lower slopes can be covered using a clear series of forest tracks. Be warned that the ascent of Binn an Choire Bhig is quite difficult and is subject to change as the path becomes more and more eroded. This is really a walk to be covered in clear weather, as foul weather could make it quite treacherous in places.

**a**   Start on the R344 road, just north of the Inagh Valley Inn between Recess and Kylemore. There is a stand of forest bearing the sign Coill Dhoire Chláir. Cross a stile beside a gate and follow the forest track downhill. The track crosses a river on two bridges, using an island as a stepping stone. There are fishery paths to right and left, but walk straight along the track, away from the river, passing a barrier gateway in the forest. There are glimpses of Derryclare Lough between the trees, but later these are lost.

**b**   When a junction of tracks is reached, take the track on the right, which rises and descends gently to another junction. Take the track to the left, which rises a little, then descends with a view ahead to Binn an Choire Bhig. Cross a concrete bridge and climb gently, then descend and gradually swing to the right. The track finally turns left and runs to an end at the

**START/FINISH:**
At the entrance to a forest on the R344 road just north of the Inagh Valley Inn. There is space for a car to park at the forest gate, but do not block the access. Patrons of the Inagh Valley Inn can use the car park at the inn.

**DISTANCE:** 8 miles (13km).

**APPROXIMATE TIME:** 5 hours.

**HIGHEST POINT:**
2336ft (711m) on the summit of Binn Chorr.

**MAPS:** Harveys Superwalker Connemara; OS Sheets 37 & 44.

**REFRESHMENTS:**
Off route near the start and finish point at the Inagh Valley Inn.

**ADVICE:**
While practically all of the routes in this guidebook are easily reversed, the ascent of Binn an Choire Bhig could be awkward as a line of descent by walkers unfamiliar with the mountain. The route is particularly rough and rocky, needing great care with route-finding in poor visibility.

Looking across the Inagh Valley to Binn Chorr, Binn an tSaighdiúra and Binn an Choire Bhig.

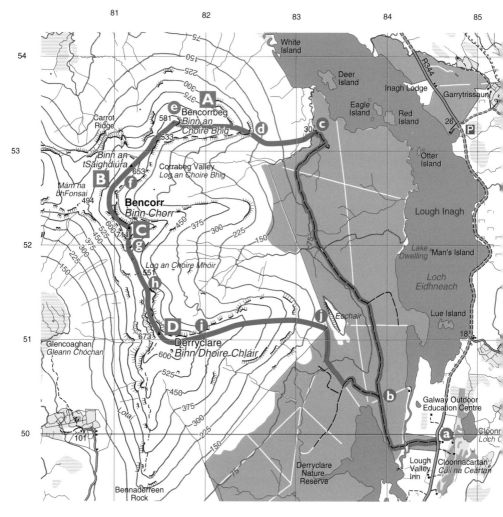

edge of the forest. It is possible, with care, to exit left from the forest before the end of the forest track is reached.

**c** Cross the forest fence and a stream, then walk up a boggy, grassy slope towards the towering form of Binn an Choire Bhig. Take careful note of two lighter coloured patches of bare rock, with a dark path cutting steeply between along a vegetated strip. Climb towards this path, which is revealed as a steep, overtrodden route on a strip of boggy ground in a quartzite gully. Tread warily, ensuring that good hand and foot holds are used. The first stretch is the most dodgy and unstable part, and those who are able to cope with steep rock should switch onto the rock to avoid wearing the path any further. The upper parts are slightly less steep, though more of the walking is on solid rock, leading to a rocky shoulder with a view ahead to the dome of Binn an Choire Bhig.

**d**  Pick any route along the rocky crest. It is best to aim left of the rocky dome, walking up steep rock slabs rather than wrestling with the bouldery slope further to the right. Little tufts of grass and heather barely cling to life on the rocky slopes, though there are other species of note: juniper, crowberry, thrift, clubmoss. There is a gravelly path towards the top, leading to a small cairn.

### A  Binn an Choire Bhig 816533
Anglicised as Bencorrbeg, Binn an Choire Bhig is the Mountain of the Small Corrie, referring to the corrie to the south of the summit. There is a small cairn on the summit dome of rock at an altitude of 1908ft (577m). Views take in part of the Twelve Bens, most of the Maum Turk Mountains and other features further away.

The rocky dome of Binn an Choire Bhig is reached after a very steep and rocky climb from Gleann Eidhneach.

**e**  Looking ahead, the rounded ridge is a jumble of rock outcrops and boulders, with patches of grass and heather. There is a trodden path, which is at best intermittent, crossing two gaps separated by a rugged hump. The next ascent is steep and rocky, scattered with stones, but not too difficult. There is a cairn on top of Binn an tSaighdiúra.

Looking along the rocky ridge towards the summits of Binn an tSaighdiúra and Binn an Choire Bhig.

## B  Binn an tSaighdiúra 812528

Binn an tSaighdiúra is the Soldier's Peak. According to local tales, a soldier assisting with the Ordnance Survey by taking distant sightings from the higher Binn Chorr in clear weather, fell from this summit to his death. The height of the mountain is 2145ft (653m).

**f**  The rocky ridge becomes a roller-coaster. The way ahead is stony at first, with cushions of thrift, then becomes more bouldery and features clumps of St. Patrick's cabbage. There are broad slabs streaked with quartz, then a path runs up a broken ridge to a small cairn. Continue to a larger cairn a short way down along the ridge, from where there are fine views around the Gleann Chóchan Horseshoe. Drop down a short rock wall to the left and continue along the ridge towards Binn Chorr. Cross slabs, then make a blocky, bouldery ascent to the summit cairn, where St. Patrick's cabbage can be seen growing, and ravens flying overhead.

## C  Binn Chorr 812522

Binn Chorr is Anglicised as Bencorr and means the Rounded Mountain. It is the highest point gained on this walk with its summit reaching 2336ft (711m). Views are quite extensive, embracing Cashel Hill, Roundstone Bog and Errisbeg. Tracking round the Twelve Bens reveals Binn Leitrí, Binn Gabhar, Binn Bhraoin, An Chailleach, Meacanach, Binn Dhubh and Binn Bhán. Dúchruach and Maolchnoc mark the position of Kylemore. Next come Mweelrea, Sheeffry Hills and Binn Gorm. The Maum Turk Mountains include Leenane Hill, Binn Bhriocáin, Cnoc na hUilleann, Binn Idir an Dá Log, Binn

Chaonaigh and Binn Mhór. Cnoc Lios Uachtair stands solitary in the Inagh Valley, with Binn Dhoire Chláir being seen last, and being the next objective on the route.

**g** Walk down from the summit on a bouldery slope, picking up a path on scree in places, with the gradient easing later. There are a few little drystone shelters on the lower rocky slopes, before the path reaches a boggy gap.

**h** Climb uphill on a gravelly path, maybe looking out for examples of highly contorted rock. There is a summit of bare rock with a cairn. This is the first of three summits on the ridge, followed by a pool and the actual summit of Binn Dhoire Chláir. The path is fairly clear, despite crossing so much bare rock.

### D Binn Dhoire Chláir 815511

Anglicised as Derryclare, Binn Dhoire Chláir is the Peak of the Oak Plain. Its summit cairn stands at 2220ft (675m). Perhaps the small oakwood protected as a nature reserve beside Derryclare Lough is a semi-natural remnant of the once more extensive oakwood from which the mountain took its name.

**i** Leave the top of Binn Dhoire Chláir and walk down a rocky slope bearing an intermittent path. The path runs between broken ribs of rock and is steep at first, though the gradient eases on a slope of broken rock and boulders. There is another steeper slope of grass and heather, with inclined slabs of rock. Walk downhill on either surface, aiming to land on a boggy gap before the small summit of Eochair, which is just inside the forest below.

**j** Cross a stile at the corner of the forest fence and follow a muddy path through closely planted trees. Despite fallen trees, clear-felling and old branches strewn across the path, the way down to the forest track is clear enough. Turn left to follow the forest track past a hut. The forest has a margin of mixed trees: alder, ash, birch, willow, and bramble. Turn right at a junction of tracks, following a track which was used at the start of the day's walk. The track runs close to Derryclare Lough, crosses two bridges over an island in a river, then climbs back up to the R344 road near the Inagh Valley Inn.

After descending from Binn an Dhoire Chláir, the little ridge of Eochair is encountered above the forest.

# GLEANN CHÓCHAN HORSESHOE

**START/FINISH:**
Ben Lettery Youth Hostel. Parking is available on a loop of old road serving an old bridge just to the east of the hostel.

**DISTANCE:** 10 miles (16km).

**APPROXIMATE TIME:**
6 hours.

**HIGHEST POINT:**
2336ft (711m) on the summit of Binn Chorr.

**MAPS:** Harveys Superwalker Connemara; OS Sheets 37 & 44.

**REFRESHMENTS:**
Nothing on the route. The nearest places offering food and drink are the Connemara Heritage & History Centre towards Clifden, Paddy Festy's at Recess, or the Ballynahinch Castle Hotel.

**ADVICE:**
This is a rough and tough walk, requiring hands-on scrambling in some steep and rocky places. The first stretch, to Binn Bhraoin, will probably take half of the time allowance.

O ne of the most exciting mountain walks in Connemara, if not in the whole of Ireland, is the Gleann Chóchan Horseshoe. A series of outstandingly rugged mountain summits around a deeply-cut glacial valley are linked by high-level ridges, or separated by awesome gaps with flanks of bare rock or bouldery scree. Complete vegetation cover is limited to the lower slopes, though there are all sorts of nooks and crannies near the summits in which a range of plants cling for survival. Overhead, ravens soar on the thermals, their croaking calls breaking the silence of the stones.

**A   Ben Lettery Youth Hostel 777483**
The Youth Hostel is ideally placed for the walk around the Gleann Chóchan Horseshoe, situated as it is at the foot of Binn Leitrí beside the main N59 road. There is parking close to the hostel where a loop of old road crosses an old bridge.

**a**   Facing the Youth Hostel, turn left off the end of the driveway and cross a stile over a fence. Walk straight uphill, passing a strip of conifers, then climbing through a band of oak and hazel planted across a bar of rock. Cross another fence to reach the open slopes of Binn Leitrí.

**b**   Pick a way straight up the steep, grassy, boggy, rocky slope, using vague paths wherever these are spotted. The slope is unremitting, so take breaks from time to time and enjoy the view which opens up across Ballynahinch Lake, revealing Roundstone

In a view from Binn Bhán, cloud brushes across the summit of Binn Bhraoin, with Binn Ghleann Uisce beyond.

Bog, Errisbeg and Cashel Hill. Look for the snipe and ravens. By drifting slightly to the left, a couple of cairns might be spotted on a shoulder of the mountain, and a braided series of paths are more easily located. Follow any path up the steep, heathery, drier, rocky slope to reach the top of Binn Leitrí. There is a prominent cairn on the summit.

### B Binn Leitrí 775495

Anglicised as Benlettery, and also recorded by the Ordnance Survey as Bendouglas, Binn Leitrí is the Peak of the Rough Hillside, rising to 1904ft (577m). The summit cairn stands on shattered blocks of quartzite. The view takes in most of the Twelve Bens, but not Binn Bhán, which is the highest in the range. The historian Roderick O'Flaherty must have been to this mountain when he wrote of 'the twelve high mountains of Bennabeola, called by marriners the twelve stakes.' He highlighted one in particular, commenting that 'Bindowglass is the highest of them, and, next the lake, is two miles high.' While not being quite so high as two miles, Bindowglass has been equated with Bendouglas, which is another name for Binn Leitrí. He also said that it 'hath standing water on the top of it, wherein they say if any washeth his head, he becomes hoare.'

c Walk along the crest of the mountain, following a vague ridge path across a broad, stony, heathery gap. A short climb uphill leads past a prominent cairn, followed by another little gap. The ground then rises more steeply and the gravelly path picks its way up a blocky, rocky slope to reach the summit cairn on Binn Gabhar.

The rocky crest of Binn an tSaighdiúra, with the rugged Binn Dhubh and Binn Bhán beyond.

### C Binn Gabhar 783507

Binn Gabhar, Anglicised as Bengower, is the Peak of the Goat. It is an outstanding, steep-sided mountain easily spotted in many views. Its rocky slopes rise to 2184ft (664m).

d Leaving the summit of Binn Gabhar, look down towards the next gap and locate a cairn on the slope. From this point, look for traces of a trodden path leading downhill and follow it carefully. There are five rocky places on the descent where hands will need to be used, though there are plenty of good holds. Always look downhill for evidence of a trodden path before making a move. Taken slowly and steadily, there should be no problems getting down to the gap between Binn Gabhar and Binn Bhraoin. With attention focussed closely on blocky outcrops, damp gullies, nooks and crannies, look out for small colonies of bilberry, crowberry, thrift, St. Patrick's cabbage and prostrate juniper – all occupying safe havens away from grazing sheep.

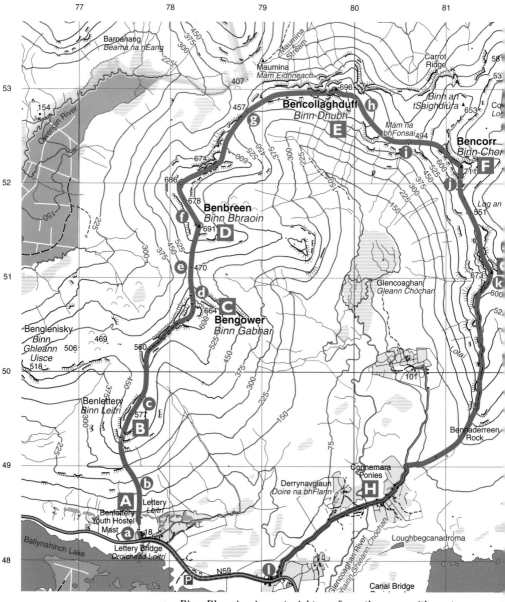

e   Binn Bhraoin rises straight up from the gap, with a steep slope of scree. Most walkers stay on a fine, worn tongue of scree, but there is better purchase for feet on the more stable, bouldery scree to the left. Even so, the ascent is a punishing treadmill of around 750ft (230m) before the summit cairn on Binn Bhraoin is finally reached.

**D    Binn Bhraoin 783516**
Binn Bhraoin, Anglicised as Benbreen, appears to be named after someone called Braoin, but folklore records nothing about who he might have been. Its height is 2276ft (691m).

**f**    Continuing along the broken, rocky ridge, there are a handful of cairned summits to pass. Some walkers climb all of them, while others skirt round them on the Gleann Chóchan flank. When navigating in mist, note that the ridge is curved, and that there is another change of direction required to reach a gap at the head of Gleann Chóchan. There is a vague, trodden path down ribs and slabs of rock, ending with a grassy slope peppered with rocks on the final run down to the gap. This is the lowest gap on the circuit, at 1475ft (450m), but the neighbouring gap of Mám Eidhneach is slightly lower.

**g**    Climb straight uphill from the gap on steep and broken rock, noting that there is 820ft (250m) of climbing to the next summit. The ascent comes in three stages, along a vague series of gravel paths, with definite shoulders in between. The last climb is particularly rocky, requiring the use of hands, though there are plenty of holds. The broad and bouldery summit of Binn Dhubh bears a prominent cairn.

**E    Binn Dhubh 798530**
Binn Dhubh, Anglicised as Bencollaghduff, is the Black Peak, rising to 2280ft (696m). The name might have been applied by early inhabitants of Gleann Eidhneach as the steep, rocky, northern slopes seldom catch direct sunlight.

**h**    Leaving the summit cairn, walk downhill at a gentler gradient, crossing bouldery ground, ribs and slabs of rock, then an extensive area of bare quartzite before reaching a narrow notch in the ridge. The notch is cut in bare rock, but is filled with soft blanket bog at around 1640ft (500m).

**i**    Cross the notch and climb more bare rock, then use a series of steep paths on rocky ground. There is a cairn on a rocky shoulder, where a short diversion allows fine views along the length of the Inagh Valley, backed by the Maum Turk Mountains. The cairn stands on a rock bar, and moving further along the rocky ridge there is a broad, tilted slab of rock to cross. A steep and bouldery ascent finally leads to the summit cairn on top of Binn Chorr.

Looking back around the Gleann Chóchan Horseshoe from Binn Dhoire Chláir, with Binn Dhubh prominent.

### F  Binn Chorr 812522

Binn Chorr is Anglicised as Bencorr and means the Rounded Mountain. It is the highest point gained on this walk with its summit reaching 2336ft (711m). Views are quite extensive, embracing Cashel Hill, Roundstone Bog and Errisbeg. Tracking round the Twelve Bens reveals Binn Leitrí, Binn Gabhar, Binn Bhraoin, An Chailleach, Meacanach, Binn Dhubh and Binn Bhán. Dúchruach and Maolchnoc mark the position of Kylemore. Next come Mweelrea, Sheeffry Hills and Binn Gorm. The Maum Turk Mountains include Leenane Hill, Binn Bhriocáin, Cnoc na hUilleann, Binn Idir an Dá Log, Binn Chaonaigh and Binn Mhór. Cnoc Lios Uachtair stands solitary in the Inagh Valley, with Binn Dhoire Chláir being seen last, and being the next objective on the route. Binn Chorr is the highest 'nail' in the Gleann Chóchan Horseshoe. Curiously, each 'nail' on the round so far has been higher than the preceeding one. The last 'nail', Binn Dhoire Chláir, bucks the trend and is lower.

**j**  Walk down from the summit on a bouldery slope, picking up a path on scree in places, with the gradient easing later. There are a few little drystone shelters on the lower rocky slopes, before the path reaches a boggy gap.

**k**  Climb uphill on a gravelly path, maybe looking out for examples of highly contorted rock. There is a summit of bare rock with a cairn. This is the first of three summits on the ridge, followed by a pool and the actual summit of Binn Dhoire Chláir. The path is fairly clear, despite crossing so much bare rock.

### G  Binn Dhoire Chláir 815511

Anglicised as Derryclare, Binn Dhoire Chláir is the Peak of the Oak Plain. Its summit cairn stands at 2220ft (675m). Perhaps the small oakwood protected as a nature reserve beside Derryclare Lough is a semi-natural remnant of the once more extensive oakwood from which the mountain took its name.

**k**  Follow a ridge path away from the summit, crossing broken, stony ground on a path which is a bit vague at times. There is a descent onto a shoulder bearing a cairn, then another descent onto a broad, hummocky, stony area. There are almost aerial views down on the huddle of little farmsteads in Gleann Chóchan, and fine views along the length of Derryclare Lough too. A worn, peaty path can be slippery on a steep slope, but the gradient eases below. At some point, where there is a clear view downhill, turn right to complete the final part of the descent across an uneven slope of boulders and bog to reach a narrow tarmac road. Turn left to follow the road out of Gleann Chóchan. The road twists and turns, passing turf cuttings and the lower farmsteads.

### H  Connemara Ponies 800405

While walking out of Gleann Chóchan, look out for Connemara Ponies. These are best described as being small horses. The Connemara Pony is a tough breed well able to cope with life in rugged Connemara. It is said that native ponies bred with horses and ponies from Spain and Morocco to produce the distinctive stock. The breed was almost lost in recent decades, but careful stock selection has retained and developed its traits. Lord Killanin is a notable supporter of the breed. Colours range from grey, through many hues of brown, to black. They are considered friendly and easy to handle, a favourite with children and possessed of an intelligence that favours them for dressage and show events.

On the descent from Binn Dhoire Chláir, there are views across Gleann Chóchan to Binn Bhraoin.

**l**  The minor road rises to join the main N59 road. Turn right along the main road. The road runs gently downhill to cross a bridge, where a former bridge lies just upstream. Benlettery Youth Hostel is just to the right across the bridge.

# FACT FILE

The following names, addresses and telephone numbers should enable walkers to track down details of any services they need.

Telephone services within Ireland: Operator assistance is available by dialling 100. Directory enquiries for numbers within Ireland is 1190. Emergency services – Gardaí (Police), Ambulance, Fire, Coastguard, Mountain Rescue – are all contactable by dialling 999 or 112.

## TOURIST INFORMATION

Ireland West Tourism, Áras Fáilte, Victoria Place, Eyre Square, Galway, Co Galway. Telephone +353–91–563081. Fax +353–91–565201. Open all year. Accommodation booking service, maps and guidebooks.

Tourist Information Office, Oughterard, Co Galway. Telephone +353–91–82808. Fax +353–91–82811. Open all year. Accommodation booking service, maps and guidebooks.

Tourist Information Office, Galway Road, Clifden, Co Galway. Telephone +353–91–21163. Open April to September. Local information service.

## TRAVEL

Iarnród Éireann, Ceannt Station, Galway. Telephone +353–91–564222. Rail services to and from Galway city from Dublin and other points on the railway network.

Bus Éireann, Ceannt Station, Galway, Co Galway. Telephone +353–91–562000. Bus services from around Ireland, between Galway and Clifden, Clifden and Leenane, Leenane and the Maum Valley. Reduced level of service in winter. Referred to locally as the CIE bus.

Connemara Bus, Recess, Co Galway. Telephone +353–95–51082. Bus services between Galway and Clifden, Clifden and Letterfrack. Reduced level of service in winter. Referred to locally as Michael Nee's Bus.

## OTHER USEFUL INFORMATION

Connemara Safari, Sky Road, Clifden, Co Galway. Telephone +353–95–21071. Fax +353–95–21797. Freephone 1800–777–200. Guided walking holidays.

Galway Outdoor Pursuits Centre, Inagh Valley, Co Galway. Telephone +353–95–34667. Specialising in outdoor education for youngsters.

Connemara National Park, Letterfrack, Co Galway. Telephone +353–95–41054/41006. Fax +353–95–41005. Visitor centre, nature trails, audio visual show and guided walks.

Kylemore Abbey and Walled Gardens, Connemara, Co Galway. Telephone +353–95–41146. Fax +353–95–41368. Visitor centre, nature trail and audio visual show.

Leenane Cultural Centre, Leenane, Co Galway. Telephone +353–95–42323. Visitor centre, Sheep and Wool Museum and audio visual show.

Ballynahinch Castle Hotel, Recess, Co Galway. Telephone +353–95–31006. Fax +353–95–31085. Historic building and hotel, with woodland and lakeshore walks.lising in outdoor education for youngsters.

Ballynahinch Castle Hotel, Recess, Co Galway. Telephone +353–95–31006. Fax +353–95–31085

Connemara Walking Centre is based in the beautiful coastal village of Clifden, located on the very Western fringe of Europe. It is a region steeped in myth whose various landscapes have been lived in for seven millenia. Archaeologist Michael Gibbons organises holidays exploring rugged mountains, treading softly on orchid rich bogs and visiting remote islands.

For further details, please contact:
Michael Gibbons
Connemara Walking Centre, Clifden, Co Galway.
Telephone +353–95–21379 Fax +353–95–21845
Email walkwest@indigo.ie
www.walkingireland.com